Memoirs of a Seafarer

CAPTAIN IAN TEW

© Captain Ian Tew 2018

Captain Ian Tew has asserted his rights under the Copyright, Design and Patents Act, 1988, to be identified as the author of this work.

First published in 2018 by Titwillow Publishing.

ISBN: 9781731222329

TABLE OF CONTENTS

MEMOIRS OF A SEAFARER	1
THORNS BEACH	6
SCHOOL	9
BOATS	12
PANGBOURNE 1956 – 1960	15
CADET 1960	25
DARA 1962	28
AFTER DARA: 1962-1964	39
SECOND MATE'S TICKET	46
INDO CHINA	50
H BOATS	58
HOMEWARD BOUND	61
ANATINA	64
MARY HELEN	66
MASTERS	68
MY FIRST COMMAND	69
ANATINA	71
BANK LINE	73
ANATINA	76
INDO CHINA AGAIN	79
SHORE JOB	83
NEW LIFE SALVAGE. SALVALIANT	87
SALVIKING MY FIRST COMMAND	113
SALVALIANT IN COMMAND	119
SINGAPORE	144
UNIQUE MARINER	147
BARGE PASTEE COLOMBO	150
STATESMAN / SALVANGUARD	156
LLOYDSMAN / SALVISCOUNT	168
SALVAGE MASTER	175
SELCO SOLD / LARGEST SHIP IN WORLD	180
NAME AT LLOYDS	183
MANAGING SELCO	185
IRAN IRAQ WAR	189
BANKRUPTCY	194
DUBAI	197
UK ALDERNEY RIO DUBAI	214
UK SHOP	218
CIRCUMNAVIGATION	222

MEMOIRS OF A SEAFARER

Master Mariner, Salvor, Yachtsman

I was born in 1943 on the day the Germans dropped a bomb on Bournemouth, that well known industrial city. Not that I knew anything about it, but I sometimes wonder if the bang has affected me!

My earliest recollections are of the sea, the water at the edge of our garden. At the age of three I was in hospital to have my appendix out. I was taken from the ward to the operating theatre fully conscious, because in those days there was no nice injection to lay one out. I have recently made the same trip and the operating theatre for this fully grown adult was a daunting place, what it was like to a three-year-old who knew they were going to cut him open I cannot imagine. I have the vividest recollection of a bright light above me and a great monster of a man pushing this rubber mask over my face. I can smell the rubber to this day. I screamed in abject fear for I thought they were killing me.

I was in hospital for six weeks. My parents nicknamed me their Belsen child for the horrors of the concentration camps had emerged. It is difficult to believe I was ever skinny, let alone skeletal, for I have always been fat.

My parents were, I suppose, well-to-do, although we never seemed to have any money and the lament was always the lack of it; but I suspect that is the same in every household however rich or poor! I was talking about this the other day with my mother to find out what she thought our position in society was.

"And I suppose you would say we were upper middle class," I said.

"No middle about us, my dear," she replied, in a tone which brooked no reply, and that just about sums it up.

I am sitting on my yacht in Tahiti typing this and England seems far, far away; and the England of my childhood seems, in time, as great as the distance I am now away. Whatever anyone might say England is rich, the roads are full of cars and the shops are full of goods.

In 1946 England was on her knees economically, reflected in the rationing then in place. A lot of things which are now part of life were simply not available or were strictly rationed. Although I knew nothing about it, being too young, I felt the effects. England was grey and shabby.

In 1948, when I was five, I had scarlet fever. It was a traumatic experience for a five-year-old, because I was sent to an isolation hospital and for three weeks lived in a glass cage. My parents, when they visited, could only wave from outside the glass; no hugs and kisses. I refused to leave my teddy bear behind, after all he had been my only companion, and I kicked up such a fuss that they fumigated him so I could bring him home.

We lived in Lilliput, Poole, in the county of Dorset. Our house, *Waterfront* was on the water's edge overlooking Brownsea Island in Poole harbour, an idyllic place to live for a child who apparently had salt water in his veins. The sea, oh the sea, it has been the love of my life, giving me my living and given me my greatest pleasures.

The house was two-storeyed, with a garage and quite a large garden with lavender along the short drive. The lavender sticks in my memory because I was either pushed or fell into it so often.

The sea was at the front of the house. At high water the beach was covered and the water lapped against the sea wall. When the tide was out there was all that lovely, gooey, sticky, Poole mud to play in.

Boats have been with me all my life. The first time I went out on my own (whether it was with or without permission I do not remember) I ended up caught by the pier that ran out down tide of the house. I was trying to sail. The first boat that I owned was a little, flat-bottomed rowing boat about 6 feet long painted red – "Redshell". My elder brother, Donald, owned a much superior boat called "Cockleshell", superior in that she was a sailing dinghy. She is featured in Eric Hiscox's first book *Cruising Under Sail*. Both boats were built at Newmans in Poole, the yacht yard my father was the manager.

I went to a 'dame school' run by old – well, she seemed old to me – Bertha Brown in Canford Cliffs. The only thing I remember was being told I was using the India-rubber the wrong way. The mistress promptly did it the same way and ruffled the paper like me.

My mother used to sail with a Miss Brotherton who lived with her father in Canford Cliffs. They had a big house with a large garden on the cliff overlooking the sea. She was a large lady and to me seemed very severe; but I sometimes went to the house, and the old man used to take me for a drive in his Rolls-Royce, which was great fun.

In 1951 my father became the manager of the Berthon Boat Yard in Lymington and we moved to Brockenhurst. Why anyone wants to live in Brockenhurst I cannot think, unless they need to be near the railway station. All the fast trains to London, except the Bournemouth Belle, stopped at Brockenhurst, so it is a rich commuter station.

My parents rented a large house on the little river that runs down to Lymington, opposite the Balmer Lawn Hotel. The house – now turned into flats – was owned by Jack Giles, the famous yacht designer of Laurent Giles and Partners. My father worked with Mr. Giles before the war when the Vertue Class yacht was designed and again during the war, on the midget submarine design.

I went to the local state school with Edward, my younger brother, and hated it. It was not very far away and we bicycled there and back in the days before heavy traffic. The highlight of my stay was getting heat-stroke and being very sick. I was in bed for days in my darkened bedroom – for the house was big enough for us all to have our own rooms. At this time there were four of us: Donald, my elder brother by three years; Edward, my younger by 18 months; and Malcolm, who was born in 1947.

The river, which must have been a nightmare for my parents, was a source of never-ending excitement to us. It flooded in winter and was nearly dry in summer. The banks in most places were heavily wooded so full of beasts and monsters – well, the new forest pony or a stag can be a frightening apparition to a young child.

My first commercial venture with Donald was at Mavis, which was the name of the house. In the spring primroses grew in profusion along the road and in the forest. The idea was for us to pick and sell bunches of the flowers to enhance our meagre pocket money. I ended up picking the flowers and selling them but Donald ended up with the money!

We were only there a year before my parents had the good fortune to find Thorns Beach and buy the remaining 33 years of a 99-year lease from Beaulieu Estate. My mother was in funds for her mother had recently died.

My grandfather and grandmother on my mother's side lived in Stawell Village, Somerset, near Bridgewater. In fact my grandfather, apparently, owned most of it. They lived in the Manor, a three-storeyed house fronting the road running through the village. My uncle, my mother's eldest brother, lived in another three-storeyed house – Manor House. My Godfather, my mother's youngest brother, lived further up the village on a hill in the Rosary, a house owned by my mother who sold it to him when he married.

The farm workers lived in farm cottages all owned by my grandfather; and Nellie, the family maid, lived opposite the Manor in yet another house owned by him. All the gentry houses and church were on one side of the road running through the village, while the farm workers houses, packing station and workshops were on the other. One of my cousins now lives in Nellie's old house, a sign of the vast changes in society since the war!

We occasionally visited my grandparents, a three-hour drive from either Poole or Lymington, and I sometimes stayed, when my grandmother was still alive. She was very keen on caravanning. I enjoyed staying in the caravan which she kept on the hill opposite Manor House. It overlooked Sedgemoor below and the River Parrett to the right – a magnificent view on a clear day.

She imparted one piece of wisdom which I have never forgotten. "Do not forget, Ian, God is always watching you even when you are alone." What mischief I had been up to for this stricture to have been made I do not know!

My grandfather, although I did not realise it at the time, was a famous man, especially in yachting circles. He sailed his yacht "Emmanuel," a 30-foot gaff cutter, across the Atlantic in 1936. He was the first man to sail single-handed from Ireland to Newfoundland and it attracted much attention at the time. The family mansion on the other side of the hill from Stawell was sold to pay for the boat.

Just before the war he crossed the Atlantic with my aunt, and then on across the Pacific to New Zealand. They were unable to complete the planned circumnavigation because war broke out. He was forced to sell the yacht "Caplin" and returned to England by merchant ship. My aunt returned three years later.

He was an aloof and imposing man to me and, according to my mother, did not like children. My chief memory of him is striding down the village in his plus fours with a large walking-stick, looking neither to the left or the right. In the Manor I was as quiet as a child can be so as not to annoy him.

After the war he did no more sailing, taking up botany as a hobby and being a Labour Council member. I particularly remember him one day in the dining-room sitting at the table – now in the house of my brother Edward – studying a plant in a microscope, the sun streaming through the window. I was quiet as a mouse so as not to disturb him.

THORNS BEACH

Thorns Beach was a paradise on earth for children, and I am beginning to think the same as a middle-aged adult. Thorns is hidden away down two and a half miles of un-metalled road on the coast of the Solent. Its 30 acres is fronted by 300 yards of private beach, inaccessible to the public unless they trespass. There was a five-acre orchard, the Barn and five houses above the road; a five-acre field, a marsh, a walled garden, a bandstand and four houses below the road. The rest was woodland.

When we first arrived there was no mains water or electricity. Power was supplied by our own generator situated in the walled garden. The garden was run by two gardeners who just about paid for their wages by the produce produced – luxuries, such as early strawberries, being sent to Covent Garden for sale.

We first lived in the Barn, which originally had been the stables and coachroom. The stable hands lived above. It was a huge wooden house: the coachroom being used to house dinghies in the winter; a large stone-flagged kitchen with a coal fired Aga enabling us to eat in the warmth; a dining-room with the table from Stawell for formal occasions; a play room; and a work room for my mother. There were seven bedrooms upstairs – one for each of us four boys, my parents' room, a room for the au pair girl and a spare room for guests. There were two bathrooms and a lavatory with a basin downstairs. Outside there were stables for four or five horses, and garages for ten motor cars! My mother did not like it for it was not by the sea, which was 100 yards away.

It was about this time that my sister, Maureen, was born. She only lived nine months. My sister was in hospital for a short while, and it was a terrible evening when my father told me she had died and would not be coming home. The funeral was a sad affair, with old Mrs Cook from the farm following us to the cemetery out in the country.

That was the end of the Barn. On the beach there were three large rooms, all that was left of a 55-room bungalow. The original bungalow was built by a Mrs Peach who kept horses in the Barn. Bands from London played in the bandstand behind the house, while 35 servants looked after the guests.

There was a road between the house and the beach and, so the story goes, Lord Montagu used to drive his cars along the road sometimes accompanied by King Edward. Unfortunately, Mrs Peach objected to the cars, saying it frightened the horses. The car driving did not stop so Mrs Peach had all the horses shot and departed. The lease was sold on to the Constants, who used to own a tramp shipping company. Unfortunately, Mrs Constant did not like the tin bungalow so Mr Constant had it all pulled down, except for three rooms, and built a two-storeyed house next door about half a mile away.

The three remaining rooms were huge but there were no usual offices. My parents built on a bathroom, two lavatories, a galley in one of the rooms and a sitting-room in the front. The house was raised about 3 feet off the ground and was built of wood with corrugated iron outside and on the roof. It is situated in a small bay almost imperceptible from the ground but clearly visible from the air, and thus is sheltered from the prevailing westerly winds. It is the only house along the shore without double-glazed windows. In the summer of 1952 we moved in and have been there ever since. (Sold in 2005 after my mother died.)

The views from the sitting-room are like images in Wordsworth's 'Daffodils' in my mind's eye. You can almost see out to The Needles in the West and Cowes, Isle of Wight, in the East. The view is ever-changing with ships, yachts, ferries, fishing boats, the occasional warship, a tug, sometimes with a tow, dinghies, canoes – in fact almost any kind of craft you wish to name – passing down the Solent with the beautiful scenery of the Isle of Wight as the backdrop. The foreshore is, of course, in a continual state of change with the tide always on the move, so whenever one looks it is different. When the mud and shingle are uncovered there are always birds feeding winter and summer. The colours are always changing with the weather – sun and rain, cloud or part cloud, wind or calm.

As a young boy the place was a continual source of wonder. There was something new to find: the bamboo grove; the old lily pond; the rock garden, hidden away down the back drive; the wood, with all its shrubs and rhododendrons; the ditch, where the old cable ran; the marsh, with its potential danger of falling into the water; and, of course, the mud; the orchard; the green field; the little orchard by the sewerage pumping station; the Windmill behind the old school house; the foreshore with its flotsam and jetsam at high water, and the mud and seaweed, rocks and pools at low water; the walled garden, an everlasting source of discovery with its growing of vegetables, the greenhouse, the seedling frames with their glass covers; the generator room with its noisy engine; the cottages with their different tenants; and the dinghies on the beach; swimming in the summer – a true paradise.

SCHOOL

I went to the local village school at Beaulieu which I loathed even more than the place at Brockenhurst. Edward and I had to walk the one and a half miles to the main road to catch the school bus, and back again in the afternoon. I expect if it was raining my mother drove us! The school was run by a sadistic head teacher who revelled in beating, and he picked on a black boy who seemed to get it every day.

Donald, now 11, was at the Dragon School in Oxford, the school my father had attended when he was a boy. I was due to go there and I could not wait. I am often told that I wrote to the headmaster, Jock Lynham, who was there with my father, and asked if I could come early. He agreed. My first term was the summer of 1952, and my ninth birthday was during the term.

Teddy Hicks was my housemaster. He was later to be a famous yachtsman and once Yachtsman of the Year.

Donald had been in the same house, so my parents knew the Hicks well. Teddy appeared to be a strict disciplinarian but I don't know if this was really the case. I once did a trip with him and his wife Phil – who did not really like boats – from Teddington Lock to Lymington in his Dragon "Gerda". "Gerda" was a very famous boat, having been sailed across the North Sea from Norway. The chief memory I have of this trip is being seasick and waking up to find that Teddy and Phil had rowed the yacht from Beachy Head to Newhaven in a calm. I felt so ashamed that I had not helped! I suppose I was ten or eleven at this time.

The Dragon was a unique school. There were few rules and so the discipline was good. What rules there were were mainly obeyed! The masters were all called by their nicknames: Jock the headmaster; Hum, his father, was still around and looked after the Sunday service; Chris Jacques was Jacko, form master of Upper One, which dizzy heights I never achieved;

Mike Gover, Gov, was in charge of Upper Two A, which is as high as I reached. Gover later became deputy headmaster many years after I left together with Keith Ingram, Inky. Mr Plummer, Plum, had the next house up the road from Teddy. Mr Parnell, Parny, took me for geography and field expeditions. I last saw Parny at my Godson's confirmation. Mr Barroclough, Putty Nose, took me for something but, more importantly, he took me – along with Nigel Forman, one of the few friends I made – to see the start of the Tall Ships Race from Start Point. We spent the night with Nigel's parents in their house at Torquay.

When I moved to School House Ma Kay was the matron. Mrs Senior did not have a nickname and took me for music lessons, at which I had no talent whatsoever. I suspect she did not much care to teach someone who was so useless.

Morning prayers were held in the Old Hall, which was there when my father was. Then there was the central hall with classrooms leading off around it. The sing-song at the end of term was held in the hall.

The New Hall was used for school plays – Shakespeare in the summer and Gilbert and Sullivan in the winter terms. Much as I wanted to I never made it in a school play! There were classrooms on the ground floor and the hall was above. I once read one of the lessons at a Sunday service, and had a small part in a film which was made.

The summer term was the best. The River Cher, which ran at the bottom of the extensive school grounds, was my favourite place. When in School House, instead of the cold plunge early in the morning taken by Jock, we ran down to the river for naked swimming. Once the clothes test was passed, we were allowed alone down by the river.

I was no good at cricket, being fat. Teddy Hicks started a sailing team and I sailed for the school.

Donald was still at the Dragon when Edward turned up so, for a term or two, there were three of us at the school. We saw the parents at half term only, although I believe you were allowed out three times a term, but petrol rationing was in force. It was with great excitement that we used to wait at the bottom of Bardwell Road and watch for the car.

My parents had a caravan which they parked in a quarry – much cheaper than a hotel and more exciting.

Donald went on to Canford. I think my parents thought we ought to be at separate schools. Hugo Moresby White – later in life to become 2nd Sea Lord – whose father my father knew, went on from the Dragon to Pangbourne Nautical College. Hugo turned up one day wearing his uniform and I thought, that looks good, I would like the same. My mother, who always wanted one of us to follow her father into the Royal Navy, encouraged me and so my fate was sealed. I went to Pangbourne.

It was many years later, at a Royal Cruising Club annual dinner, that I heard my mother tell Richard Devitt, the grandson of the founder, that they had made a mistake. But it is no good blaming circumstances, least of all parents who are doing the best they can. And, of course, at that stage I did not know it was a mistake. Over thirty years later I obtained my old school reports and on opening the first one, realised that, indeed it was a mistake. I was far too individualistic to be a good Naval Officer

I never made friends easily, and very few at that. I only remember Nigel Forman and Andrew Scorah from the Dragon but I kept up with neither after leaving, although I wrote to Nigel when he became an MP and when he was made personal private secretary to Lord Carrington, but I never received a reply! I had even stayed with him at Torquay with his parents to watch the start of the tall ships race. I know Teddy Hicks was quite disgusted with him when he was at Oxford for staying in Linton Lodge, the hotel near the school run by Tony Retty! I have no idea what happened to Andrew.

BOATS

My mother owned "Mary Helen", a six-ton gaff cutter my father designed and built with the proceeds of their wedding presents in 1936. She spent the war in a mud berth in the Beaulieu River but they now sailed her each summer cruising to France. Just before the war they cruised west around Great Britain to Norway and back via Holland, for which my mother had been awarded the RCC Challenge Cup – the first lady to win this cup. It was not won by another woman for 50 years.

We sailed with my parents unless farmed out – whether we liked it or not. Luckily I liked it and so do all my brothers. So the sea, boats and sailing have been and continue to be, an all important part of my life. I am sitting here in Tahiti on my 39 feet yacht typing this, having started to sail around the world!

The first boat I owned was "Redshell", and how she ended her life I do not know. I know I had her at Thorns Beach. The most important thing about my next boat was that she was a proper sailing dinghy. My father ordered two Lymington Scows 11 feet 6 inches long built at the Berthon, one for me and one for my elder brother Donald. "Titwillow" was mine and she was painted yellow and I loved that boat. She was given to me on my eighth birthday which was in the summer of 1951. During the summer she was kept on the beach at Thorns where I sailed her. In the winter she was kept in the Barn where I painted her.

The next year I visited Beaulieu River and Lymington River, but Lymington was marred by the Isle of Wight ferries which appeared huge in the narrow river. The marshes to the west were intersected by Pyewell Creek and if the tide was high enough I could sail through to Tanners Lane and Pitts Deep almost half way to Thorns. It was great fun to sail through the marshes, with the smell of the esparto grass, and if the tide was not high enough, the smell of the mud.

In the Easter holidays I used to collect seagulls' eggs and

sell them to Fishy Foot, the fishmonger. On windy days, with a fair wind, I would run through the creeks causing a huge wash in the narrow channel, especially if the tide was not full, imagining I was a pirate escaping the Navy, or a smuggler outsailing the Revenue Cutter. On calmer days I would sometimes take a picnic and glide through the creeks.

I first sailed across the Solent when I was ten. The Solent is a narrow waterway between the Isle of Wight and the mainland and being narrow, the tides are strong. With a westerly wind and ebb tide the sea very quickly gets up the famous Solent chop. I think my parents were very brave and in today's world of rules and regulations, I would think they would be considered irresponsible. I heard in later years that they would sometimes be seen at the club looking out for me on a rough day. I knew nothing about it; as far as I was concerned, if I was allowed to do something I was expected to do it properly.

I sailed all over the Solent and to Cowes for ice-creams. They were the creamiest I have ever eaten.

Newtown was a fascinating place to explore. Once I was in Newtown and the weather deteriorated the wind increasing so much that at the narrow entrance I realised it was too rough to sail home. I enlisted local help to leave the dinghy, somehow got myself to Yarmouth and caught the ferry to Lymington – all with no money! I always carried money with me after that incident!

Lymington was the more exciting river to sail because of all the traffic, even in those days before the marinas. Every half an hour or so I had to contend with the ferries. The Royal Lymington Yacht Club held their summer regatta in which I used to participate. My father manned the Berthon yard launch as a rescue boat. On one race where the course took us out into the Solent there was a fresh breeze. I was eleven or twelve at this time and I lifted the centre plate when running downwind. My father told me to put it down to stop the rolling but in my infinite young wisdom I knew better and capsized. What an ignoble end to the race, but it was the only time I ever capsized my scow. I sailed in pretty strong winds, even reefing at times, and often had to bail but they were remarkably seaworthy dinghies.

There was a day regatta at Hurst Castle at which I raced, and at Yarmouth, Isle of Wight. I once sailed over for the race only to find it cancelled due to the bad weather, so sailed back again to Lymington in disgust.

PANGBOURNE 1956 – 1960

Pangbourne was a complete and utter culture shock from the freedom at the Dragon School and the freedom of sailing in the Solent, with the responsibility and self reliance it brought. I entered a world of rules and regulations, cadet captains who could and did beat other boys, petty regulations, uniforms and all the triviality it entailed, of being correct and above all of having to conform, having to be like other boys. But I was not like other boys, I was me. Other boys did not own their own boats, and I did not want to conform. I was fat and combined with my nonconformity, I was the butt of much bullying 'within my own peer group', according to the report.

We used to go by train to the Dragon School but for my first term at Pangbourne my parents drove me. I can remember the excitement. I wanted to go to this school, I wanted to join the Navy, I wanted to do well.

Port Jackson, the house all of us were in for the first year, was set in the most lovely grounds just down the hill from the main school. Once my parents departed the veneer of civilisation was off and I entered the world of discipline enforced by the older boys with the full concurrence of authority. It was an alien and utterly strange world where everyone was considered to be stupid, or that was the way it seemed.

'Accers', the early morning run, was a nightmare. Whatever the weather, when the bugle sounded at 06:30 you had three minutes – or was it five? – to wake up, dress in running gear and parade outside, there to be told by a cadet leader or cadet captain where to run. They would follow on a bicycle. I was not a fast runner and tended to bring up the rear end. Well, if the boy in charge felt sadistic he, in the name of discipline, would order the last boy home to go round again. This made you late for everything. Someone had to be last but, of course, the maxim was to make sure it was not you. A bit like flogging the last man off the yard in the days of sail.

Once home you were hosed down by the cadet leader with a cold hose and if he was feeling playful he would aim the strong jet at your genitals, which you were not allowed to protect with your hands. The cold water bit was no problem, being used to Jock's cold water plunge, but the other was more difficult to handle. It was all in the name of toughening you up for the rigours of life – to be men, to be leaders in the dying days of the British Empire. It was the last gasp of a system that had stood the empire well, but turned out to be an anachronism in today's world; the empire was already dead and its system outmoded. Maybe I should not complain, I survived. Even if I wanted to do something about it I could not; it was too late I was there, and my parents were making tremendous sacrifices to send me to a decent public school.

Survive I did. Whether by accident or design, I cannot say. If you cannot beat them join them and conform, and this I did to survive – but only after much pain and effort. No doubt it could be said the system worked in my case, certainly my life would have been different if I had attended a normal school.

In my first year I had to box, whether I wanted to or not. I did not. I have always considered boxing to be totally barbaric in a civilised society. Well, being fat, I was a heavyweight and so got beaten up in the ring by a well-developed elder boy and the so-called match was stopped before the end by the captain-superintendent. That is the one and only time in my life I have boxed.

After a year in Port Jackson under 'Minnie' Beat the housemaster – who I never knew, presumably because I kept out of official trouble – I moved to Hesperus Division. The housemaster there was a very different kettle of fish. His name was Holland and his nickname was The Brute. And he was not called The Brute for nothing. He ruled the house by fear and no one escaped at least one beating while in his house. Mine was two weeks before I left in my last term, but I am ahead of myself.

The divisional building was a concrete monstrosity with concrete floors and cold as sin in winter with those old-fashioned, upright, iron, steam radiators. I once visited Alcatraz, the infamous island prison in San Francisco Bay. Standing in the old dining-room, having walked round the prison, I had the most horrible feeling that I had been there before; and it was some time before I realised that it was Pangbourne.

The Brute used to prowl around at night to catch people talking after lights out and give them a beating, or at least this is what he seemed to do. Every month there was a report – or maybe it was every two weeks – from the masters in charge of each subject and if you got enough betas it was a beating. Often the victims were beaten in the evening and when it was over in would come The Brute to take evening prayers. He was a tall man with a strong face and he walked with his head poked forward.

The summer term was the best. The school owned a number of Fireflies and sailing was considered a sport, so I had a chance to excel. The sailing was run by Bobby Aitken, assisted by Cecil Rogers who owned National 12 12-foot dinghies. The boats were kept on the bank of the Thames next to the school rowing boathouse. It was on the reach where the famous Swan Inn is situated, mentioned in Jerome K Jerome's *Three Men in a Boat*.

The sailing stretched one's sailing ability, however much wind was blowing, because it was so fluky with trees on one bank and a hill above the other. Bobby Aitken was much the organiser. A short man who bustled about while Cecil – who was not very fit, his blue face giving away his heart condition – was just there issuing instructions in a high-pitched voice.

On my second summer, when I should have made the first team, one of those school disasters occurred. The rowers always considered the sailors to be sissy and wet, while the sailors considered the oarsmen to be all brawn and no brain! I was crewing with Ewen Tailyour, later of Falkland fame. An eight was just pulling off the bank when Ewen mimicked the cox in a falsetto voice which I stupidly copied. Ewen was the Captain of Sailing so I got the blame. The Executive Officer Ronny Hoyle, who was in charge of rowing, heard us. There was no love lost between Hoyle and Aitken and I was banned from the river for the summer. Bobby either would not or could not do anything about it so I had no sailing that summer and so missed out on the chance of being Captain of Sailing in my last summer. Rodney Pattisson, later of Olympic fame, whom I regularly beat racing, was captain. How important school honours seemed at the time, and what desolating disappointment when one missed out! The next year I did make the school team and was awarded my colours.

On my last summer The Brute refused to make me captain of the house team because I had not been promoted, making chief cadet captain Rae, who was useless, captain instead. I threatened to refuse to sail for the house which, no doubt, annoyed The Brute. God, how it hurt!

I was entered for a Royal Naval Scholarship at the age of 15 and had to go to London for the interview. My parents arranged for me to stay with Roger Pickney who was a prominent member of the RCC. I went to London by train in my uniform and found my way to the flat, which was an excitement in itself having previously only been to London en route to stay with my Godmother. He took me out to dinner at a Greek restaurant which made me feel very grown up.

The next day I reported on board HMS *Wellington*, sat some sort of intelligence test and in the afternoon was interviewed by three men. I failed so dismally that I was not required to go for the weekend of activity tests. Thirty years later I read the report Pangbourne sent to the Naval Authorities and knew why the interview was such a waste of time – I had no chance. Maybe it has turned out all for the better but at the time I was deeply disappointed and considered myself a failure. The young, or at least I did, feel hurt and pain just as much as the adult! Many years later my youngest brother James won a Royal Naval Scholarship, so honour is satisfied as far as the family is concerned.

***

Founder's Day was the big occasion for parade work. We were trained up in our marching and spruced up our shoes so you could comb your hair in the reflection on the toe cap. I would wait for the great day with much trepidation that I would not do something awful like fall over or faint or turn the wrong way. A prominent person from nautical life would be the guest of honour. The one I particularly remember was Captain Sorrell, who was captain of the *Queen Mary* and had docked her in New York without a pilot or tugs – which was considered a great achievement. He, would make a speech, and the captain-superintendent would make a speech and then the prizes would be given. I actually won a prize, or maybe two, for 'industry', never for being first.

People like Ian Phillips, who was handsome, one of the best-looking people I have ever met, brilliant at sport and never seemed to have to make an effort scholastically, usually won. I was a 'plodder'. The only thing I was good at, and really enjoyed, was sailing; but in those days you could not make a living out of sailing.

Was I happy? Did I enjoy my school days? To be utterly truthful I really do not know for I am not sure what happiness is. To begin with it was an endurance test to survive, but once I thinned down and the peer group bullying stopped I tolerated it. The thing that stands out most in my mind is that I wanted to achieve, to be amongst the best, but only ended up top of the second division. The one area where I did achieve – sailing – I came out top, although Hoyle's arbitrary banning still rankles even after all these years.

I went to an old boys' reunion dinner the other day, the first time in 36 years, (which says a lot about how I felt about the college) and sat close to Ewen Tailyour. When I reminded Ewen of the episode with the rowers he pretended not to remember but, after the wine had flowed a little more, he did remember and apologised. And I feel better as a result. Pathetic, really, but that's life!

***

My last term – the summer of 1960 – was a nightmare. I was not promoted, which I thought I should have been. Many of my term intake were already promoted but I, in my own mind, considered I was as good as them if not better but I was only in the Merchant Navy form and the top people went into the

Navy, then the Army, then Civilian Life and lastly into the Merchant, even though the place was founded for training officers for the Merchant Navy.

Devitt and Moore were a famous sailing shipping company in their day. They ran a cadet ship and later founded Pangbourne Nautical College to train boys to become officers in the Merchant navy. If you put in charge of such an establishment passed over Royal Navy captains, what do you expect? Captain Lewis was the captain-superintendent at this time and he had an unprintable nickname. He had the typical boozer's ruddy complexion – or maybe I am being unjust and it was a heart condition – I can only write what I thought and felt at the time.

As I discovered when I got the old reports from Pangbourne, my card had been well and truly marked. I had complained to my parents that we were not being taught maths properly because the master was ill or sick and only an older boy was taking us. The class was a shambles and I was learning nothing. Being that earnest young adolescent who wanted to get on it was not good enough. My parents duly complained to the school. The Director of Studies, a dry old stick called Topliss, who used to smoke a pipe, investigated. Although he agreed with me, Authority was not going to admit I was right so my parents were fobbed off with a half truth letter and, more importantly, I was marked as a trouble maker. In those days you simply did not moan, not least when you had a retired Royal Naval disciplinarian at the helm.

***

Two of the privileges I achieved were a bicycle and the use of a senior boy's room at the top of the division. Two cadet captains were caught drinking in the Red Lion pub and had been disrated. The Brute called me in and said that my privilege of using this room – oh so important to a schoolboy, both for 'face' and to get away from the hurly-burly of the gunrooms, or recreation rooms in civilian parlance – was withdrawn. I was dumbfounded with shock and protested vigorously but much good it did me. The Brute had not yet beaten me, I so far had evaded his cane. It was so utterly unfair and unjust. I was the 'good' boy, I had done nothing wrong, yet here were two boys who had been promoted and broken the rules and I was getting the punishment for it. It cast a complete cloud over my last term and the humiliation of having to return to the gunroom, the sniggers and looks. However, I still had my bike and used to go for long rides.

My parents came up on a Saturday to take me out – I suppose there had been no sailing match – and combined it with a visit to the Dragon School where my brother Malcolm was a senior boy. We returned from Oxford and were having dinner at the hotel in Streatley by the River Thames. My father wanted to finish his wine so we would not be back by the 20:00 deadline, however senior boys with permission were allowed out till 21:00. I had not asked for this permission although, being in my last term, was entitled to this privilege. I was back before 21:00 and my father said, "If there is any problem tell Mr Holland to give me a ring."

Some weeks later The Brute called me into his study and said, "Mr Stephens," – who was the deputy housemaster – "tells me he saw you in the hotel at Streatley after 20:00. You did not have permission to be out that late." And he grunted, his stock-in-trade, and puffed on his pipe.

"That is correct, sir, and I apologise for not having obtained permission for the extra hour but we had not expected to be that late. My father requests that you ring him if there is any problem," I politely replied.

He grunted and dismissed me. At first I could not see what I had done wrong but realised that it might have been more prudent to have got my father to come in when I was dropped off. I had forgotten the first rule of survival – 'if you infringe a rule, however stupid, cover your arse!'

The Brute's grunt presaged trouble but I assumed he would ring my father. The term dragged on but The Brute's grunt still rankled. He was the past master in the art of fear, and the longer I heard nothing from him the worse my fear became. It was like Kafka's novel *The Trial* – what crime had I committed? No one would tell me and I was being tried without knowing what the crime was.

I imagined all sorts of scenarios and the worst one was that he would take away my bicycle. I was deeply unhappy in this, my last term. Its one saving grace was my bicycle because it gave me freedom of a sort and of course, 'face' amongst the juniors. The tension became unbearable and like the antihero in *The Trial*, I was ready to submit to anything.

At long last the call came and I turned up at his study. The door was shut. I knocked. Silence. Shall I knock again, has he heard? The Brute really was the ultimate in perpetrating psychological fear.

I had almost plucked up courage to knock again for there was no point in antagonising him.

"Enter."

I heard the grunt. I opened the door and went in. He was sitting in his armchair facing the door. I closed the door behind me and stood to attention in front of him. There was no pipe.

"I am going to beat you for impertinence," he said.

No preamble, nothing, he had got me. But, as in *The Trial*, The Brute could have done anything to me and it would not have mattered for the one thing that really mattered was still mine – my bicycle. I was so relieved I almost smiled, but my face remained unchanged.

"Take out your shirt from your trousers and bend over that chair."

It was almost with eagerness that I complied. He took a little run and administered the first stroke. My head was singing 'I still have my bike' as the second stroke fell, and then the third, and then the fourth, 'hell, it's going to be six but I don't care, I've got my bike,' the fifth and then the final sixth stroke fell.

"You can go now," he grunted.

I turned, looked him in the eye and said, "Thank you, sir, goodnight, sir."

He dropped his eyes looking so surprised that I thought he was going to say something, it was obviously not the reaction he was expecting. I quickly left, tucking my shirt into my trousers. I was 17 and later reproached myself for not having fought him, but I was so relieved at keeping my bicycle. I never told my parents. It was rumoured the Brute beat a boy for being late back while his parents were still outside the building, I certainly believed it true.

It was two weeks to the end of term and the days dragged into an eternity. Eventually I went down to the village and telephoned my parents to come and take me away before I went mad. This, in itself, was a crime. You were not allowed to telephone without the housemaster's permission. I was due to join my first ship with British India in a few weeks and I could not stand wasting time with the pettiness of Pangbourne, especially after the Brute's psychological success.

***

My father always considered Captain Lewis to be a scruffy individual. I don't know if they had some disagreement, maybe it was the maths. Anyway I was called in to see Captain Lewis, presumably for him to wish me well for the future, and his parting words were, "Don't let your father say things against me," and to this day I never knew what it was all about.

My parents came to pick me up four days before the end of term. The Brute never said goodbye and the last time I saw him he was scuttling round the corner of the building as we drove up the drive. Maybe he thought I was going to complain to my father about the beating, but I was far too relieved to worry about that. He was killed in a car crash (or maybe he died of cancer) about seven years later, and when I heard I did not mourn. I recently read his glowing obituary in an old copy of the school magazine and did not recognise the man I knew as my housemaster or divisional tutor.

And so I left Pangbourne with its imposing main building set on the top of a hill with the most glorious views over miles of unspoiled countryside, trees and green fields; its own magnificent grounds; the long drive, at the sides of which – at the beginning of the summer term – were carpets of bluebells; the woods, where hidden schoolboy trysts took place; the magnificently kept playing fields, where battles between the schools were fought in rugby and cricket; and, above all, the river with its sailing and rowing on a beautiful stretch of the Thames. It was 36 years before I visited the river again. The boathouse was there, the whaler and a launch but it was not the same. There were no people. Where was the passion, the hurt, the competitiveness, the striving to achieve, the absolute necessity of defeating the other person sailing; the winning? I sailed for the school in the Public School Boys' Championships on the Gareloch in Scotland, near Glasgow. It was held in Dragons and Garelochs. I did well two years running and was due to go for my last year. However, my father said I should go to sea on the date specified by British India and my mother argued I should sail for the school. My father won.

***

I was 17 and two months old when I left school and entered the adult world, and it was almost out of the frying pan and into the fire. But then, that is life and it is up to you what you do with what life throws at you. An old friend of my parents, General Richardson, when he was old and blind after an active life – including sailing – once said to me, "Ian, your parents have given you the tools to equip you for life. You are an educated person; I cannot tell you a course of action is right or wrong, it's up to you to make that decision. You know what is right and wrong, but when you have decided stick with it."

CADET 1960

I joined the British India Steam Navigation Company Limited (BI) cadet ship "Chindwara", and it was a mistake! This was a new world but one that I was not prepared to accept because the systematic bullying of first trippers was wrong with a capital W. I could not just accept what was happening and leave it. The Dragon School and Pangbourne had taught me that and it had been reinforced by General Richardson. I decided on my course of action and followed it through.

The bullying started on the first or second night in London when the senior cadets came back from the pub. All the first trippers were rousted out of their bunks and lined up along the bulkhead. A boy, well young man really, well built and tough, called T was the worst, he punched everyone many times in the chest. I really cannot remember how much it hurt, it was the humiliation. Pangbourne had been a pretty tough place one way or another, and I simply was not prepared to be beaten up by a bunch of drunken bums. Not all the senior cadets took part, but those who did not did nothing to stop it. It went on all the time we were in London and was known as Sports Nights. Once at sea it stopped.

The ship was on BI's East African run. Barclays District and Colonial Bank (DCO) were strong on that coast. My father knew the chairman of the bank, and the managers of the various branches were warned I was on the way. In Port Sudan the captain of the ship received a message that a car would pick me up – which it did – and off I went to dinner. This treatment, much enjoyable though it was for me, did not endear me to the other cadets on board, least of all the senior bullies.

In Massawa the bullies came back drunk from the brothels and a 'real' Sports Night took place. We were all rousted out and, after the initial beating, locked into the drying room with the heat turned up. There were 12 of us in a very small hot space and Massawa was a hot place without being in a drying room. I tried to rouse the rest of the first trippers to fight back. There were enough of us to take on the bullies but I could not persuade them, even though one of them had been at Pangbourne with me but in a different division. His name was J and he was quite good-looking. We were individually taken out of the drying room and ran the wet towel gauntlet – naked except for underpants. Once back in the drying room I again tried to rouse the rest of them to fight back, but to no avail.

The 'sports' went on for some time and ended up with us hanging on a pipe to see who lasted longest before falling off and receiving more towel flicking. At some point J's underwear was pulled off and either he or someone else was forced to put an irritant liquid on his genitals.

I wrote to my parents explaining what was going on and asked them to do something about it. They did. They went to see the chairman of BI – they had an introduction from a fellow director.

Meanwhile we sweated our way down the coast – air-conditioning was a thing of the future – visiting Aden, Mombasa, Zanzibar, Dar Es Salam and Tanga. All the places were British, the 'wind of change' – the famous Macmillan words in South Africa – had not blown on this coast yet. The ports were all run by the British and the key posts were all held by expatriates, even down to the ship's stevedore foreman.

How well run the ports were run. Everything worked, and good loading and discharging times were obtained by the African labour. I was taken out by the Bank Managers in both Mombasa and Dar Es Salaam. They all had lots of servants and after the cadetship it was great to be waited on. After Tanga the "Sports Nights" stopped. My parents visit to the Chairman had taken effect. Once the other Cadets discovered who had blown the whistle, I was sent to Coventry. The other first trippers on pain of a beating were forbidden to talk to me. It is quite difficult to live in silence, the only communications were instructions from the senior cadets about work and such throwaways as "beware of the shackle from on high" or "we will throw you overboard in the channel" and other intimations of a violent death. "The Brute's" psychological training in fear may have helped me for I survived the voyage intact. A Mr Spanton joined the ship in Gibraltar to investigate my allegations and I was interviewed by him. I do not know the outcome of this enquiry but I was transferred to another ship. Once more out of a sizzling frying pan into an even deeper fire.

DARA 1962

I was to join the deck passenger ship "Dara" in Bombay. My father took me to the airport which was a new experience for me and I think for my father. My luggage was so grossly overweight that I had to repack on the floor at the airport and he took half my stuff back home. The aircraft was the modern up to date jet a Boeing 707. I watched with alarm as we took off, the wings flapping in the breeze up and down while the great jets underneath moved from side to side. I thought my last moment had come and the thing would break up on the ground, but lift she did and flew me to Bombay via numerous stops on the way.

Nothing in my past prepared me for India, less than twenty years after independence, the noises, the heat although it was winter, the hordes of people, the slums, the poverty, the smell and the beggars. I made it a rule for life never to give to a beggar on the principle if you gave to one you were morally bound to give to all. Who were you to play God. It is said you either love India or hate her, there is no in-between. I loved her. Just as well, as it would have been difficult to have remained otherwise. It was completely different from Africa.

The "Dara" was a deck passenger ship of 5,000 gross tons and she carried about 1,500 passengers on deck, a couple of hundred in second class and 30-odd in first class. The cadets, along with all the European officers, ate in the first class saloon – a different world from the cadet ship.

There were only two of us and I shared the cabin with the other cadet, Josh Grimwood. The cabin was situated on the officer's deck down a short alleyway from the chief officer's cabin, a far cry from the dormitories on the "Chindwara." Josh, a European Kenyan from the white highlands, was the tough senior cadet. We got on well enough, and he was very good at showing me the ropes for I was still pretty green despite the voyage to East Africa.

Here we were, young officers under training as opposed to trainee able-bodied seamen (ABs) to work the ship. The only time I had been on the bridge of the "Chindwara" was as trainee quartermaster to steer her. Here my station – going in and out of port – was on the bridge dressed in whites. My job was to answer the telephone and relay the orders from the captain and pilot and write up the bridge bell book – a pretty responsible job for a 17-year-old!

We even had a 'boy' to look after us, clean the cabin, clean our uniform shoes, and make sure we had clean whites from the laundry. Domestics taken care of! A bit different from England.

***

Captain Elson was a man of few words. Chief Officer Jordan was a thin man but I had even less to do with him than the captain. Josh, being the senior cadet, dealt with the mate. The second, third and fourth officers were the watch keeping officers and I only saw them when I was at my stations entering and leaving port. I mainly saw the third officer whose station was also on the bridge.

There were two radio officers – an elderly man and a youngish second – to work the wireless telegraphy and tap out all messages in Morse code. We had almost nothing to do with the engineers who lived in separate accommodation aft on the boat deck. The cadets had their own table in the only air-conditioned place on the ship – the first class dining saloon. The rest of the crew were Indian. I was supposed to learn 'Malim Sahib's Hindustani' but regret to say I never did.

The "Dara" – along with the three sister ships "Dumra", "Dwarka" and "Daressa" – ran a weekly service from Bombay to Basra via Karachi and gulf ports, sometimes calling at two ports in one day. Although I did not know it at the time, I was serving a dying company on routes made possible by the empire, also in its death knell.

It was with much trepidation that I went to the bridge for my first stations. Josh had showed me around the bridge and how the telephones worked – by setting a dial for whom one wished to speak to and cranking a handle. The bridge seemed crowded with the pilot – still, there was an Englishman – his Indian assistant; the captain; the third officer; myself; and two secunnies, one to steer and the other to run errands, hoist or lower flags or relieve the secunny at the wheel. The captain's boy was always on hand for coffee, tea or cold drinks for the Burrah Sahibs.

I was in a funk to start with. The ship had to be manoeuvred out of the docks and through the lock gates into the harbour. There were numerous orders to relay and reports to be made from forward and aft, but I soon got into the swing of it and began to enjoy myself. This was the place I wanted to be – on the bridge at the control centre! I was required to record every engine movement, so remained alive and alert the whole time.

Stations going in and out of Bombay always took a long time, and once out of the dock we went alongside Ballard Pier to load the passengers and mail. Ballard Pier was near the 'Gateway to India', the great archway symbolising entry into India. The departure of the weekly mail ship to Basra was an event. The ships were the only way to get around most of the Persian Gulf at this time so we were an important link between India, Pakistan, Oman, Gulf States, Saudi Arabia, Kuwait and Iraq for the travelling public. The ships were always full of passengers.

Sailing day from Ballard Pier was a day of hustle and bustle. The shouts and babble of hundreds of people with their wives, children and servants; the cries of the porters carrying the luggage, huge bundles on their heads; and the street traders hawking their wares.

The cadets loaded the mail. Well, we did not carry anything, we supervised it – together with the second officer who was in charge. To lose a mail bag was unthinkable.

There was a steady stream of humanity coming aboard via the gangways; shouts and sometimes scuffles as men staked out part of the deck for the voyage. Of course, the more privileged went second class and enjoyed cabins. Europeans were not allowed to travel on deck. First class came on board by a separate gangway where the duty secunny kept watch.

The tween decks, where the deck passengers lived, seemed a

form of bedlam to me on my first Gulf trip. There were two holds forward in the ship – both for passenger baggage and for cargo – and the winches were working full speed swinging the cargo on board by the derricks, the stevedores sweating in the holds stowing it.

At long last everyone and everything was on board; the ship was fully bunkered and watered; the trip to the money changer completed, for there was a nice little earner exchanging Indian rupees into Gulf rupees and up the Gulf the other way round; not that I had riches to spend. My first year at sea I was paid £3 per month which came out of the Bond my father paid for me to be apprenticed to BI.

The pilot was on the bridge; the tugs made fast fore and aft; the gangways were put ashore; and, with much shouting, wailing and waving from the passengers on board and the families left ashore, the ship moved off the berth. She was turned and the tugs were let go. With a last blast on the ship's foghorn, the "Dara" steamed out to sea through the busy harbour criss-crossed by country craft with their ragged sails or if there was no wind with their crews toiling at huge sweeps, all laden with cargo for trading up and down the coast and when the monsoon was fair to East Africa. We passed anchored ships waiting for a berth – the buildings of Bombay to starboard – and so out into the Arabian Sea and up the coast to Karachi and being the North East monsoon the weather was fine with a calm sea.

The ship at sea was a world of her own and, apart from the noise of the diesel engines, it was quite quiet. If my duties took me down to the tween decks there was the continual babble from the hundreds of passengers in the vicinity and it was sometimes difficult to get through the decks because the passengers spread themselves and their belongings.

The sea routine was very pleasant. We looked after the lifeboats and checked the gear, water and food – not that we ever expected to use them. We changed into whites for all meals and were expected to be in the saloon on time. When off duty I studied and worked at the correspondence course we were expected to complete.

The distances between the ports were quite short, especially in the Gulf, so we were in and out of port most days. I particularly remember Dubai because we anchored off, as we did for most ports in the gulf in those days. The passengers were taken ashore by barge towed by a tug, but we went ashore in the agent's launch and landed in the creek. The creek was full of dhows loading and unloading their cargoes; on the port side, entering the creek, were the stalls and shops where duty free goods of all kinds could be purchased. Dubai was the centre of gold smuggling to India.

We spent a few days in Basra, being the other terminal port from Bombay, but there was not a lot to do ashore for an impecunious cadet. Bombay was much more fun with swimming at Breach Candy – the swimming club where girls might be met. The club in those days was for Europeans only.

I managed to get a sail or two at the Royal Bombay Yacht Club in Seagulls hired from the club, but it was expensive for me and I had to tip the boatman who crewed for me. The tides run strongly in Bombay so local knowledge was useful.

Josh introduced me to the delights of the cages in Grant Road where Ladies of the Night sat in barred windows displaying as much of their wares as they thought necessary to entice you inside and sample them – for a fee, of course. A considerable amount of beer was consumed on board, before my first trip to Grant Road, because there was prohibition in Bombay at that time. You needed to sign on as an alcoholic before you could get a permit to purchase booze. That was impossible for me because my indentures forbade me from drinking alcoholic beverages or entering houses of ill repute. Josh was the organiser for supplies of beer on board.

***

I was in the Seaman's Club one Saturday feeling lonesome. Bombay was a long way from home and the world I now lived in was very different from England. A man started up a conversation which eventually got around to the lack of booze. He said he lived in an apartment with lots of booze and invited me up. He seemed a decent sort so I accepted, thinking nothing ventured nothing gained. Well, to cut a long story short I passed out – whether from too much drink or because something was slipped into my drink I do not know. When I came to I found myself naked in bed with my new 'friend' performing a very intimate service on me, an abomination. I was horrified, shocked and filled with disgust. I leapt out of bed, dressed and ran from the flat. When I got back to the ship Josh asked me if I was all right, but of course, I could not tell him what occurred in that flat. He was a tough East African. There was no one I could talk to, so I carried the guilt around with me. I showered and showered to try and feel clean, to cleanse myself of the shame.

***

It was April 1961 when I started my fourth voyage just after the incident with the man. The weather was beginning to hot up in the Gulf. The "Dara" was anchored off Dubai discharging cargo and passengers.

During the afternoon the wind increased and a cargo ship dragged its anchor and collided with us on the port side. There was much shouting and pandemonium, but the only damage was to the lifeboat situated between the forward holds. However, the wind continued to increase and Captain Elson took the ship to sea to ride out the storm, taking a number of Dubai stevedores with us.

It was rough when we turned in. I climbed into the top bunk, Josh sleeping in the bottom one. At about 04:00 I was awoken by the fire bells ringing. It was still rough, the ship was rolling and pitching. Josh said it sounded like an emergency and we better get up and go to our fire stations. The lights were not working so we dressed quickly by the light of a torch and went out of the cabin into the alleyway.

We met the third officer who said, "There is a fire on B deck. Go to your stations."

We went to our fire station, collecting the breathing apparatus on the way, down to B deck. B deck, which was one of the passenger decks, was complete bedlam. There were people running around in various states of dress shouting and screaming, the noise amplified by the roar of the fire which lit up the area – the light rising and falling in intensity. One man was running around screaming with blood all down his front. Josh donned the breathing apparatus and tried to get to the emergency shut off fuel valves on the engine room bulkhead on the starboard side of B deck but was driven back by the flames. Looking along B deck there was an unholy glow, the smoke masking it like a fog. There was no other lighting.

Josh said, "This is pretty hopeless, we had better go to our boat station."

We fought our way back through the jostling, screaming, panicking passengers to our boat station which was between the two aft holds, a torch our only light. It was still dark and the ship was rolling dead in the water.

We let go of the gripes and lashings off the boat so we could swing it out for lowering. Josh told me to get in because this was my boat and I was in charge of it. I climbed on board and Josh lowered the boat to embarkation level. What a panic! The strongest passengers swarmed on board.

"Lower away, Josh!" I shouted, "the boat is already full and more are trying to get on board."

He could see what was happening and lowered the boat into the water. Unfortunately, an empty boat drifted by from the boat deck forward of our position. The passengers all went to the side of my boat and it capsized. I ended up in the waters of the Persian Gulf. It was still dark and quite rough. The burning ship drifted away from me and I was on my own. I do not know what happened to the passengers from my boat.

I took stock of my position. The ship was drifting too fast for me to swim back to her. I was not wearing a life jacket – it had not entered my head to bring it with me from the cabin. Luckily I was a strong swimmer and passed the Award of Merit in Lifesaving at Pangbourne. I was still fully clothed so took off my shoes and dungarees. In my haste to leave the cabin I did not put on any underwear. Without the dungarees it was a lot easier to swim but I kept my shirt on. There was not very much I could do except tread water and wait, the occasional wave breaking over my head. I was alone with my thoughts but I was not afraid. Oh youth, immortal.

It started to slowly get light and I saw what I thought was a shark's fin not far away from me. I thought this was my punishment for the incident with the man, and the sea water was the final cleanser. I was now clean again.

I watched the fin and after what seemed an eternity, I realised that it was not moving and a little later that the fin was in fact a human body clutching an oar. The sense of relief that I was not about to die was quite overwhelming. I swam to the oar.

There was a body on the oar and I put my arm around her. It was lighter now and I could see she was not wearing a life jacket. Her face was in the water a lot of the time, the waves washing over it, her hair a black mass swirling around her head and I did not know if she was alive or dead. After it became completely light she fell off the oar and disappeared. I suppose I had been in the water for an hour and a half by this time. I have often wondered if I should have done more to try and save her, but was she already a corpse? Had I been holding onto a corpse for the last hour?

In the daylight I saw a lifeboat near by, and abandoning my oar, I swam to the boat. When climbing on board one of the passengers noticed my lack of bottom clothing and kindly gave me a pair of shorts to make me decent, for there were a few women in the boat. The assistant purser gratefully handed over charge of the boat to me. It was still rough and the lifeboat was rolling uncomfortably so I persuaded the crew and a few passengers to man the oars and keep the bow into the wind and sea. It made it much more comfortable for everyone.

Some time later it was beginning to get hot as the sun rose in the sky. A tanker appeared close by and I instructed the rowers to row. We made our way over to the ship, which had stopped in the water with the gangway down.

I told the assistant purser I did not think there was any use trying to get the women off first and just let the men go as they would. We came alongside the gangway and a reasonably organised disembarkation ensued. The men went first followed by the women who were helped up the gangway by the Japanese crew when necessary.

Once the boat was empty I found a man asleep in the bottom of the boat, face down. I tried rousing him but it was to no avail so managed to roll him over onto his back. It was then I realised it was a corpse, the string eyes. I thought the family would want the body so managed to persuade the Japanese to take the corpse on board and put him in the freezer. I finally came on board myself and the lifeboat was set adrift.

The passengers were accommodated and I was given a cabin in the crew quarters. One kind crew member gave me a bottle of whisky which I drank, blotting out the burning horror of B deck; the panic; the man with blood all down his front; the screaming; the roar of the flames; the imagined, yet very real looking shark's fin; the corpse in the water; and finally, the corpse in the lifeboat.

The Japanese tanker took us to Bahrain where a very irate agent berated me for bringing the corpse on board.

"I thought the family would want it, sir," I replied.

"Do you realise the trouble you have caused me just to get it ashore, let alone out of Bahrain? You should have chucked it overboard or left it in the lifeboat," he said.

***

The "Dara" tragedy was the biggest peacetime disaster to strike a British ship since the "Titanic" and attracted world attention in the Press. I cannot think why I was unable to communicate with my parents although, in those days, it was not a matter of just picking up the telephone receiver. I, for some reason, was left off the list of survivors and it was three days later before my parents were told I was safe. It was many years later before I was told by a brother the terrible weekend it had been waiting and wishing for news of me.

I stayed in a hotel in Bahrain where the BOAC air crew stayed; was kitted out with a minimal of clothing; issued with a passport 'original lost at sea'; and finally, joined the "Aronda" for the voyage back to India. I gave evidence to the Preliminary Enquiry held in Bombay where I was told not to talk about my experiences to other people. I flew home for my two weeks 'survivor leave'.

Johnathen Priest, my best friend at school who was still

there, had written to me whilst I was on the "Dara". He told me that Captain Lewis had called the whole school together and told them that the rumours flying around about bullying on the cadet ship "Chindwara" were completely untrue and I was a liar.

Toby Hickman, who was on the East African coast at the same time as the "Chindwara" on a Clan Line ship, was on leave. I had complained to him about the bullying when we met up in Mombasa and he said that he would rouse his 'white' crew and come over to beat up the bullies! I asked him if he would accompany me to Pangbourne and lend moral support so that I could confront the captain-superintendent. He agreed and I borrowed my parents' car and we drove to the school. I passed my driving test a few weeks before joining BI.

***

I found Captain Lewis on Big Side watching a cricket match. It was a fine, sunny day and the green, well kept grass showed up the whites of the cricketers; a very English scene. He was sitting in an armchair and I went up to him. Even though I had left the school, there were butterflies in my stomach.

He said, "I hear you did very well on the "Dara", Tew."

"Thank you, sir," I replied and went on, "I am told you called the whole school together and called me a liar, saying that there was no bullying on the "Chindwara". I assure you, sir, that everything I said was true."

"Oh, I believe you, Tew, but that is not the point. The good name of the Merchant Navy was at stake as far as the college was concerned, and for the common good I had to scotch the rumours."

I looked at him in disbelief. "We were taught here at Pangbourne to be honest and truthful in all things, yet you were prepared to lie and blacken my name for the so called good of the Merchant Navy."

"Yes, and good day to you." He ended the conversation.

I could hardly believe my own ears and walked away in a state of shock. Captain Lewis RN Retired had just undermined what I thought the ethos and teaching and character building of the Nautical College, Pangbourne, was all about. Toby almost disbelieved me. I had no dealings with the college for over thirty years, not even a letter. It is a very different place today from all accounts - well it would not have survived if it had not changed.

We dined at the Swan Inn and I drove Toby back to Sandbanks, which is just the other side of Bournemouth. It being very late when we arrived, I spent the night and overslept. I was not popular when I returned the car to my parents; they had to hire a taxi to take my youngest brother to school.

AFTER DARA: 1962-1964

My survivor leave was soon over and I flew to Calcutta to join a ship of which Henry Severs was the master. He was chief officer of the "Chindwara" on my first trip so I was hardly in his good books! The drive in from the airport was a culture shock, even after Bombay, the poverty was abject. The Hooghly River ran fast and brown but I did not notice it. I fell sick and was hospitalised.

The Woodlands Nursing Home was to be my home for over two months. For part of the time I was in a coma and I had both a day and a night nurse to look after me. I was conscious when my bladder refused to work and the matron used a catheter without lubrication or anaesthetic. I screamed in agony. It did not work and she said I would have to be operated on. I was in low spirits after my two weeks in a coma and really frightened. The little night nurse took things into her hands. She put me in a warm bath where my water works started to function again and there were no more problems. I was soon on the mend and when I was discharged I joined the "Okhla". I never knew what was wrong with me.

The "Okhla" was docked in Kidderpore Dock and she was old. She was a five-hatch cargo ship with split accommodation, driven by a steam up-and-down engine. There were two holds forward of the officer's accommodation and saloon; another hatch number three; then the engineers' cabins surrounding the engine and boiler room; with another two hatches aft for and five. The cadet's cabin was on the port side at the forward end of the engineer's accommodation; outside, within 2 feet of the end of the top bunk, was an open steam winch. When it was working, the whole cabin shuddered and shook, the noise making conversation almost impossible.

Peter Thomas was the other cadet and he was senior to me. When I arrived on board I was shocked to find him sitting in the cabin in his underwear, but any passenger ship ideas were quickly dispelled. The ship was hot as hell and it was the height of the South West monsoon, so it was not just hot but wet and sticky as well!

Peter Thomas – whose parents worked in Rhodesia – was a nice chap, and we got on well together. Captain Elson from the "Dara" had taken over as the master but was silent and withdrawn. His wife was with him. Donald, the chief officer, was a short playful Australian but being the junior cadet I had little dealings with him at first. The second officer was a large, jovial fellow and we got on well together. I used to drink illegal beer with him. The third officer was a tall, thin man called Ricky, who sometimes drank considerable quantities of alcohol and was a bit of a wild boy ashore. When he was drinking I sometimes got roped in as a drinking companion.

Calcutta was a city of brutal contrasts: wretched poverty alongside considerable wealth; slums alongside imposing colonial buildings. The streets were teeming with people and taxis with no brakes. The river was busy with a lot of country craft traffic always going with the tide, the ones filled with bricks were especially heavy to sweep when there was no wind. There were lots of small rowing boats ferrying people to and fro across the swift running muddy river.

At certain times of the year there was a bore – like the Severn bore in England – when a huge tidal wave came roaring up the river on the beginning of the flood sweeping all before it. If the agent had any sense any BI ship would be safely tied up inside a dock.

The Calcutta Swimming Club – Europeans only – was a social centre. I once saw an immensely fat man in the changing rooms being dressed by his boy and thought that was the way to live, really being waited on hand and foot!

We left Calcutta for Rangoon in Burma. The Irrawaddy River was almost as interesting as the Hooghly but not nearly as long. There were still some old European Hooghly pilots left with their own bearers and cook, but in Burma all the Europeans had gone and the pilot was Burmese. We moored to buoys in the stream and commenced loading rice for

Mauritius.

We were in Rangoon for about a month and took a full load. Peter and myself were put on cargo watch and whenever cargo was being loaded from the barges alongside, one of us was on duty. The important thing about rice was to ventilate it properly and it was our especial duty to make sure the stevedores did not skimp on placing the wooden box ventilators at regular intervals amongst the bags.

Our other main duty, apart from being on deck and keeping an eye on everything, was to place the electric lamps for cargo work at night and watch that the stevedores did not smash them. When working cargo there was continual noise from the open steam winches – slow, when heaving up a load on the union purchase between two derricks; and fast and rattling as the load was allowed to drop into the hold or the empty sling put over the side into the barge.

Even though the "Okhla" was only a cargo ship with no passengers, there was proper silver service in the saloon. We had to change into clean whites before meals and to be on time. We ate at our own table, clean white tablecloths and napkin.

The shore-going launch was driven by steam. There was a miniature telegraph in the wheelhouse which the coxswain used to manoeuvre. *Ding ding* and the steam engine would go ahead; *ding* and it would be stopped; and *ding ding ding* would be astern. The boat had been built before the First World War, but was still in perfect running order.

Rangoon – isolated from the world for years – was very run down, the beautiful colonial buildings in a state of disrepair and bare of paint. The old Strand Hotel must have been magnificent in its day but was now a shell of its former glory. Still, you could get cold beer.

The Mission to Seamen owned a club house out on the lakes which was little used. I persuaded the padre to let me take out the sailing boat they owned – with the boatman – and spent many a happy afternoon sailing in the hot sun dreaming of the Solent and Thorns Beach.

I visited the magnificent Shwedagon Pagoda with its quite

stunning views over the Irrawaddy River, and the surrounding fields shimmering in the heat of the sun. The higher I climbed, the better the view, and at the top the gold leaf on the pagoda glittered and shone in bright sunshine.

The old "Okhla" could only manage 11 knots maximum – well, say 10½ – but, deep laden, she drew a satisfactory wash on the river banks when we departed down river. Once clear of the muddy waters and strong tides of the delta, we steamed through the clear blue sea in fine weather to Mauritius. Peter and I were put on bridge watches with the officers, which I thoroughly enjoyed. I stood the eight to twelve with Ricky taking a sun sight in the morning and working out the noon position after shooting the sun at its zenith. The night watch dragged a bit on the ocean voyage, but Ricky usually gave me a beer at midnight in his cabin. He bemoaned his fate that he was on antibiotics and could not drink – the result of a wild night ashore. He soon made up for it once he was cured! Any off duty time was spent studying because Captain Elson expected us to be up to date with our correspondence courses.

Mauritius was a beautiful island in the Indian Ocean, south of the equator, unspoilt and remote from the world. There was no airport, so the only means of transport to the island was by ship. With the blessing of Captain Elson, no doubt encouraged by his wife, a party was held in Port Louis on board the ship. A lot of people turned up and the cadets were allowed to attend. All the officers and ourselves were smartly dressed in 'Red Sea rig' – long blue uniform trousers, white shirt with epaulettes and cummerbund. The upshot of the party was that the cadets and officers were invited to spend the weekend at the house of one of the guests on the other side of the island on the beach. I was one of the lucky ones to go and spent an idyllic weekend swimming and partying. I fell in love with the daughter of the house but it was in vain. I corresponded with her for some years and sent Christmas cards for many more, but it became a one-sided affair.

***

We left Mauritius in ballast for East Africa. The Indian crew refused to clean the hold bilges, so Donald ordered Peter and I to do it. What a job it was! The bilges were full of fermenting rice which had to be dug out, along with the biggest cockroaches I have ever seen in my life. If you stood on the big ones they would carry you a few yards before succumbing. The smell was overpowering and I was glad when we finished. What a contrast - eating our meals dressed in clean whites served by our boy!

On the East African voyage we went on the 'nut' run. I don't know whether it was so named because of the cargo we carried (cashew nuts) or the mental state of the people on board!

Captain Elson left the ship, Donald was promoted acting master and I was promoted acting third officer. I was 18, being paid as an officer, and secretly very proud of myself. Peter was transferred to a home line ship for leave and so missed out. The next time I saw Peter was some years later. He was in hospital in the United Kingdom and his head was shaven. He was paralysed all down one side and could not play his guitar properly or barely speak. The brain tumour from which he suffered had been operated on and he underwent radiation treatment, but it had left him partly crippled. He recovered enough to fly out to Rhodesia but dropped dead on the tarmac in front of his parents.

***

I enjoyed being third officer, and the acting second officer lent me a pair of epaulettes. On the coast we loaded a full cargo of nuts for India, the last port being Mombasa. In addition to my deck watch I had to make the cargo plan and it had to be ready before we sailed, so sailing day was a panic. It was a relief to be back at sea and standing the eight to twelve watch on my own, the old man only being on the bridge if there was a squall or another ship on a steady bearing.

We discharged all the nuts in Cochin and a new captain joined so I went back to being a cadet, which was not much fun. In Bombay I was transferred to the deck passenger ship "Kampala", so beginning my long journey home for the "Dara" enquiry.

The "Kampala" was about ten thousand tons gross and carried just over a thousand passengers – the deck passengers all having bunks. There were many more first and second class.

Together with the "Karanja", the ships ran a monthly service from Bombay via the Seychelles which did not have an airport, to East Africa, terminating at Durban in South Africa. They were the main link between the two continents before the advent of air travel killed them off. The three voyages I made were very pleasant during the fine weather of the North East monsoon. Time in port, except Bombay and Durban, was short to keep up the mail schedule. In Durban, Garner Lynham – the brother of Jock Lynham, headmaster of the Dragon – used to take me out. He had been an orange plantation owner but was now retired.

In Mombasa I joined the home line 12-passenger ship "Chilka". Why the home line ships were so different from Eastern service I don't know, but they were. Everyone was much more uptight, cadets were to be kept in their place and there was little fraternisation with the officers. I was senior cadet and the chief officer was a mini martinet. The master was 'Granny' Vincent who was actually quite pleasant.

In Tanga the other cadet and myself hired a car and drove for a day up country, which was fun and exciting. The voyage home was rough in the Mediterranean and we painted the saloon one night off the coast of Portugal.

The "Dara" enquiry was held in London and the wreck commissioner was Porgies. Gerald Darling was the QC representing BI. On the day I was to give evidence my father came with me to London. I was almost nineteen years old but it was a daunting experience to sit up there in front of a lot of people and answer questions about the tragedy and what I did or did not do.

After the enquiry I flew to Calcutta and joined the "Bulimba" – a new, fast, modern, air-conditioned cargo ship on the India-Australia run. I was the senior cadet, which I liked, and for the first time at sea in fact in my life, occupied my own cabin. or bedroom. Irene Theabold, a first cousin, used to live in India and she had given me an introduction to the chairman of Metal Box. His charming Indian wife used to invite out to formal dinner parties and dance nights at the Tollygunge Club, a very superior club just outside Calcutta.

The Gemmels used to invite me out for sailing at the Barrackpore Sailing Club where we sailed Enterprises on the Hooghly. It was thought to be dangerous to fall in the Hooghly because of dead bodies, and so sailing had only just started and was for the more hardy. No one seemed to suffer any ill effects of a capsize. I sometimes still managed a sail in Rangoon but the mission boat became very decrepit with no maintenance.

We were normally not very long in Penang or Port Swettenham, where we picked up palm oil in the deep tanks. It was the cadet's job to make sure the deep tanks were spotlessly clean and to monitor the temperature during the voyage. In Singapore I used to go out with Peregrine Bruce whose parents lived in Lymington and whose father was a well-known yachtsman. He had an MG sports car, which was fun. On the Australian coast there were parties in Perth, Adelaide, Melbourne and Sydney – the girls usually from the local hospitals – and a boozy, sexy time was had by all!

I was happy on that ship. I played bridge with the captain, AB Stephens; the chief officer, Mr Fullager; and the third officer. I drank whisky with the other two while the third mate was a teetotaller. It was a pleasant run to be on, the ship was quite new, I studied hard, and life was pretty good.

My sea time for second mates was almost up and I joined the home line ship "Woodarra". There was the same startling difference between home line and Eastern service. She was a very fast ship – a maximum speed of 20 knots – built for the wool trade, but it was not a happy voyage, and I was glad to get off in London. I had been away from England for well over a year so was glad to be back at Thorns and meet my family.

SECOND MATE'S TICKET

I went to the School of Navigation at Warsash to study for my second mate's certificate. Warsash was on the other side of Southampton Water from Thorns Beach, so was very convenient for me. I spent the weekends Ocean Racing on "Daiquiri", a Nicholson 36 skippered by Nicholas Edmiston, who was younger than me. I was 20 that summer.

On the Lyme Bay race, running back from the mark under spinnaker in thick weather, there was a cry on deck, "Breakers ahead!"

"Luff!" I shouted and ran on deck.

I was the navigator and realised that it was the tide race off Portland Bill. We sailed round it, having dropped the spinnaker and carried on to the finish. It had been an alarming moment.

Nineteen sixty five was a Fastnet year and Nicholas entered. The crew – we were all amateurs in those days – was pretty well worked up having sailed all summer together, so it was with high hopes when we started off from Cowes. My elder brother, Donald, was sailing with Ren Clarke in one of the Quivers and I thought he might easily be the winner. I was still the navigator and took my sextant with me – the days of GPS were in the distant future. We ended a respectable sixth in our class, having been the youngest crew ever in the Fastnet, and that was the last Ocean Race I took part in. I suppose circumstances conspired against me participating again and, to be absolutely truthful, much as I enjoyed the season racing with Nicholas, my heart was not in it. I preferred cruising.

I passed all the examinations for second mates, including my orals with the formidable Captain Freaker. I was a qualified officer in the Merchant Navy at the age of 21, and quite pleased with myself.

***

BI was a dying company, as was the whole British Merchant

Navy – not that I realised it at the time. As its name implied BI was tied up with India and so, as the Indians flexed their 'independent' muscles and started expanding their own fleets, companies like BI declined. I don't think management was very clever in seeking out new trades. If the Greeks could do it I don't know why we could not have done so, or perhaps tradition was so deeply ingrained they were incapable of making the radical changes necessary to survive and in the event they did not, being completely absorbed by P&O.

BI had 50 ships at this time, down from an overall total of 250 in its heyday, but had 250 second mates. The prospects for promotion were not exactly good and I was much too ambitious to want to remain a junior officer for years, so I wrote to various shipping companies and eventually accepted an offer from Ellermans.

I flew out to Gibraltar with Captain Fairhurst and the other officers and joined the "City of Oxford", a 12-passenger cargo ship, on the Canada-India run as third officer. The crew, as in BI, were all Indian. The ship was run very much as a BI home line ship as opposed to Eastern service; junior officers were not allowed to use the bar or fraternise with the passengers.

We discharged and loaded round the Indian coast but were switched to home line so ended up back in the UK instead of Canada. I had asked to sail on a Canada-India run ship so that I could get my sea time in as quickly as possible. I wanted to sit for my first mate's certificate, and leave did not count for sea time.

I did another two trips as third mate to India and East Pakistan, Chalna and Chittagong on the new cargo only "City of Worcester", joining her in Birkenhead and leaving in Liverpool. I made a UK coastal trip on one of the big four, the "City of Durban", and then joined the "City of Poona" for a trip out to the Far East as junior second officer.

This trip really broadened my horizons in more ways than one. East of Singapore was a different world. We called at Bangkok – that really opened my eyes in the world of the erotic! Labuan and Jesselton in East Malaysia; Sandakan and Tawau in Borneo; then to Hong Kong.

Navigating amongst the reefs of Borneo was fun, though no doubt a nightmare for the master. As we were going into Hong Kong a smart passenger ship was departing and I thought I would not mind joining that company.

We went on to Taiwan where the medical regulations required that a glass tube be inserted into the rear end to see if you were suffering from typhoid, or some such disease! This provoked outrage amongst the officers, but it was quite simple – no glass tube, no shore leave. The lure of exotic Chinese women won!

The trip to Hong Kong really set me thinking. I joined the "City of London" in Avonmouth. I had been promoted to second officer and my parents came up to see the ship. Captain C B Parks Bradbury was in command and he was quite a character in his own way. He wrote letters and articles for *The Nautical Magazine* about shipping. He was short and stout with the ruddy complexion that comes of good living, and had trouble with his legs. What I liked about him was that he left you alone on the bridge.

The ship was a steamer so ran silently at sea. She had recently been refitted to take Sir John Ellerman, the owner of the company, to South Africa. Sir John was a recluse and a world authority on rats, or so I had been told.

We sailed for India and East Pakistan, loading a full cargo of jute for the return voyage. We all worked hard supervising the loading to obtain a good stow, sweating down the holds in the heat.

On arrival in the UK the ship was held up by Jack Dash and his cronies for three weeks. The London docks were on strike. This finished me off as far as the UK was concerned. What was the point in sweating my cojones off in awful places like Chalna and Chittagong to get a good turn round if people like Dash could destroy it all. I would leave the UK and work abroad; but first I had to get my first mate's certificate.

It was the summer of 1965 and I had not done much study since obtaining my second mate's certificate. Junior officers in those days worked hard and there was not a lot of leisure time, especially if exotic ports like Bangkok or Keelung were visited! I studied hard and passed. I was a qualified first mate at the age of 22. I was quite happy with my progress; I wanted to be master sooner rather than later.

INDO CHINA

Through the good offices of Sir Julian Crossley, the chairman of Barclays DCO, I obtained an interview with Captain Stourmont of Indo China Steam Navigation Company Limited in London. It turned out to be overkill but I was determined to join the company, whose passenger ship I had seen leave Hong Kong on the "City of Poonal". Captain Stourmont accepted me and I signed a contract to serve for four years, after which I would be given six months home leave. Time spent waiting for a ship or sick leave did not count, so I might be away longer than four years. I was not worried, I would get my sea time for masters all in one go.

Piggy was the not very flattering nickname of the Captain of the "Eastern Star" which I joined as third mate or rather officer on arrival in Hong Kong. He was an aloof individual who kept his distance from his officers. Russ Sanderson was the chief officer and we got on well together. The ship was loading for Australia from barges alongside. Being a Jardine ship she was moored at buoy No 1 in the harbour - a prestige position. She carried 12 passengers in great comfort, with superb food and service. Officers were expected to socialise with the passengers.

The "Eastern Star" being on a liner run maintained dates and her schedule called for a speed of 15 knots between ports. She was a turbine-driven steamer and suffered from boiler problems which meant there were periodic stops at sea to fix the boiler tubes. Water was always a problem and some form of rationing was normally in effect at sea. She was air conditioned which was great.

We seemed to spend a considerable amount of time in port around the Australian coast, with continuous parties on the go, Brisbane, our first call, was normally an overnight stop which gave time to sample the local beer - after Hong Kong San Miguel on board - and eat Australian steaks. There were two calls at Sydney and the ship was moored at Darling Harbour. It was only a 15-minute taxi run to Bondi Beach which, I'm ashamed to say, I never visited. There were different girls each night for the continuous party. I am not sure Melbourne was any more sedate and Adelaide did not live up to its religious reputation. North-bound we loaded coal at Gladstone, much to Piggy's complete and utter disgust.

"We are a passenger ship not a bloody collier," he raged. It was the first time such a menial cargo had ever been loaded on a Jardine Australian run ship. We discharged it in Nagoya after calls at Osaka and Kobe, the stability being very poor having loaded it last in the tween decks, the ship rolled appallingly.

From Japan we sailed for Shanghai in the grip of the Red Guard Terror, now almost forgotten. There was a continuous barrage of communist propaganda from loudspeakers ashore 24 hours a day. Red Guards invaded and painted slogans in our accommodation and our crew were terrified. They were made to kneel infant of their interrogators in the officer's saloon and two were taken off and never heard of again. There were some hectic parties ashore in the Seaman's Club; and a night on Chinese style champagne gave me a fearful headache the next day and a raging thirst.

Back in Hong Kong I was transferred to the "Eastern Argosy" as second officer with a very different Master. Captain Sullivan joined in all the parties. The fourth mate was a live wire and he held a pilot's licence. The ship called at Port Kembla and after an all night party, we chartered a plane. The fourth mate flew three of us up to a small airport north of Sydney, where we enjoyed a beer and came back again. He even let me fly the thing.

I think there was one of the perennial strikes by which the dockers held the Australian nation to ransom when the ship was in Sydney. Some friends from Beaulieu - Commander and Mrs Borthwick and their family - were stationed in Canberra on secondment from the Royal Navy, and I flew up to spend a weekend with them. It was my first time in Canberra, a city completely different from the rest of Australia. Emma, their youngest daughter who was about six at this time, years later married my youngest brother. I was his best man.

In Adelaide I was diagnosed as suffering from a peptic ulcer. I had been coughing up blood and not feeling 100 percent. Much to the disgust of the chief officer the doctor said I should not stand a watch while the ship took me back to Melbourne and a private nursing home. The chief officer had to stand a watch!

I was given a comfortable private room in the nursing home, and after many tests and discussion it was decided not to operate. The doctor told me my style of life was not the problem, it was my attitude to life which needed to change. I was too upright, too tense and if I did not change I would be dead before I was 30. It was pretty shattering news for this ambitious person. How did I go about changing my attitude to life? Well, I must have succeeded or I would not be writing this over fifty years later.

The parents of a friend of my parents in Beaulieu lived in Melbourne. The doctor agreed I could go and stay with them in their large house in Toorak because they employed a cook and gardener and I would be properly looked after. Lady Bassett and her cook looked after me whilst I was still in bed until I was allowed to get up and move around the house and garden.

Lady Bassett was a writer and was writing a book for which I traced a map. Sir Walter, her husband, was the retired chairman of Mount Isa, a prominent mining company. He took me sailing in his boat, drove me around the countryside in his car and entertained me but no alcohol of course. I was on the wagon for six months.

They owned a weekend house on the Mornington Peninsula at the entrance to Philip Bay at the head of which is Melbourne. We spent a weekend there and I went for long walks on the almost deserted beach on the sea side of the peninsula. Two months after being diagnosed I was declared fit enough to work and returned by air to Hong Kong.

On arrival in Hong Kong I joined the "Eastern Maid", a small cargo ship on the India-Japan run with all the intermediate ports, including Bangkok and Shanghai. Captain

Parrish was the marine-superintendent, and the manager was Captain Lewis. The chairman of Indo China was David Newbigging and the company was owned by the powerful Hong, Jardine Matheson. David Newbigging later became Taipan of Jardines.

It was not long after my return before I discovered I had joined the wrong company. The company who owned the passenger ship I had seen was China Navigation, owned by Butterfield and Swire, but, no matter, I was in Hong Kong – a live, bustling place.

It is difficult to describe the different feeling between Indo China and the home companies. It is possible that the personnel were a little more adventurous, having made an effort to leave the UK. The ethos – if that is the way to describe it – was different. We all worked for the company and were looked after by the company together. In home line companies everyone seemed to be fighting 'them' in Head Office, and people were a stickler for rank. Not so with Indo China where Christian names were more likely to be used than not; unheard of in home lines.

Life on board the "Eastern Maid" was very pleasant. Full silver service in the saloon. With white tablecloths and napkins and crested silver and crockery – despite no passengers. We had wine with dinner every night. Ah Soo looked after me and the third mate only. He dealt with all the domestics, was on call night and day for cold drinks, and in port, if I went ashore, would be on hand to see if I wanted anything when I returned!

She was only a small ship with four holds, two forward and two aft, and a single tween deck but she was on a liner run with dates to keep. We loaded and discharged for the following ports: Hong Kong; Singapore; Port Swettenham; Penang; Rangoon; Calcutta; Chalna; Chittagong; Penang; Port Swettenham; Singapore; Bangkok; Hong Kong; Yokohama; Nagoya; Osaka; Kobe; Shimonoseki; Shanghai; and back to Hong Kong. The ship was never empty and it took considerable skill on the part of the chief officer to plan the cargo work so that all four holds could be worked at the same time, and no overstowing.

I was second mate and looked after the charts, Sperry gyrocompass, winding the chronometer and the navigation. I drew the courses on the charts and I don't remember the captain changing any.

I was on board for over a year with the same chief officer, captain and third mate. The crew never changed. Ah Soo was trained to bring me cold San Miguel beer when I was on stations aft near meal times. The second mate of a Ben Line ship, who was watching us berth ahead of him in Singapore, almost fell overboard when Ah Soo turned up dressed in his white No. 10 uniform holding my beer and glass aloft on a silver tray!

If the exotic and erotic girls of the East are known, it is not so easy to have wild nights out in India and forget about Bangladesh. Once the last of the Straits ports – Penang – was cleared north-bound, John, the chief officer, would lay out his Scalextric on the boat deck and long complicated races would ensue when the ship was in port. The stevedore foreman would have to wait for an answer to his query if a race was on and he came up to the boat deck. There was a suitably located bell to ring for the duty boy to bring up cold beers to keep us refreshed during the long hot afternoons.

***

Shanghai was not much fun. The Red Guards were running riot, loud speakers blasted communist propaganda 24 hours a day, and there was an atmosphere of fear in the air. The crew were terrified. Young Red Guards swaggered round the ship with rifles through our accommodation and there was nothing we could do to stop them. They would often paint slogans in the alleyways outside our cabins and the atmosphere was very different from my visit on the "Eastern Star." Ashore people looked at us but no one made any hostile move.

The Seamen's Club, with its great long bar, did a thriving business because there was not much else to do except spend money in the friendship store. They were the only two places we were allowed to visit. There was always a minder with us ashore.

The grand buildings along the bund were still there, albeit needing a facelift, but the traffic was only bicycles. I, for one, was glad to see the back of Shanghai when we left. This was the last call we made to Shanghai. The Indo China Australian run ship "Eastern Moon" was arrested, the European officers beaten with rifle butts and made to tear up the British flag. It took all Jardine's influence – which was considerable – to have the officers released and sent back to Hong Kong, while a new set were sent to Shanghai to sail the ship. Part of the deal was for the ship to go round the Australian coast with the slogan 'Hang Wilson' painted on the side.

After a year both the captain and chief officer went on leave and life changed. Ken Millar joined as master and our nice, peaceful existence was over. I was promoted to acting chief officer at the age of 23, which I was very satisfied about, acting could be turned into permanent! However, Ken was newly promoted and very much the new broom. He had difficulty remembering that he was the captain not the chief officer, so I found life a little difficult on board. Ashore he was a genial host and some fairly extensive parties ensued – not least in Calcutta where the European stevedore manager came on board for his glass of gin for breakfast! He would take us for extensive curry dinners in the evening.

On the south-bound Hong Kong call we were caught up in the riots which the Gurkhas sorted out. The highlights for me were running away from tear gas in Kowloon, ending up in some bar, and walking through the deserted streets of Hong Kong after curfew. It was very eerie to hear my own footfalls, something normally impossible in busy Hong Kong. I bribed a bumboat to take me back to the ship, and we sailed without a pilot shortly afterwards.

The next time we called in Hong Kong I was taken off the "Eastern Maid" and joined the "Ho Sang" as chief officer. This was a completely different way of life and was really a throwback to a pre-war existence. The ship was an old empire boat, built for service in the Second World War. The captain and officers' accommodation were amidships over the saloon and officers' galley. The engineers and crew were aft around the engine room, and the engine was an old steam up-and-downer. The main difference about this small ship was that we carried our own stevedores for loading and discharging cargo in Borneo. The total complement on board was 99; if we carried 100 we would have been forced to carry a doctor.

On the south-bound trip the crew were allowed to carry their own cargo on deck, for which privilege I, as chief officer, received a small payment; the captain a bigger one. The north-bound cargo was logs. The captain was 29 and I did not see very much of him except on ship's business.

Loading south-bound, although ostensibly under my supervision, was done by the Hong Kong stevedores. It was for only two or three ports so was not very difficult. North-bound the bosun was the stevedore foreman and he wanted me out of the way! I was considered much too efficient because I inspected the holds twice a day. There was, of course, a duty officer on duty at all times.

In Borneo picnicking on deserted virgin beaches was the order of the day, and the bosun could never get the boat in the water fast enough. The chief steward would make up a hamper for a barbecue and enough cold beer for the day. Sometimes guests from ashore would join us, and a jolly time was had by all.

Sandakan and Tawau were the main ports, with the occasional calls at Jesselton south-bound and Bohian Island north-bound. It was a pretty sybaritic life interspersed with a sea voyage across the China Sea to and from Hong Kong. The food on board was good, dinner at 19:30 with wine and, of course, full silver service.

The log discharge was round the back of Lantau Island, so I used to live in a hotel in Hong Kong or Kowloon. Sometimes I stayed with Graham Sneath, then solicitor general of Hong Kong.

Jardines owned two sailing yachts – "Highwayman", a Dragon; and "Jadalinka", a 30-foot cruising boat. We were allowed to hire them for a very modest fee and I took advantage of this privilege. I spent some happy hours sailing in the waters of Hong Kong with just the boatman as crew.

The yachts were kept at the Royal Hong Kong Yacht Club, of which I was a temporary member through my membership of the Royal Cruising Club. I met Graham at the Yacht Club and we became friends. He owned a Chinese junk called "Peccavi", which he kept out in junk bay at the RHKYC club house. We spent many a happy day sailing and swimming and eating and drinking.

I had not been feeling quite as well as I usually do and eventually went to the doctor. I was diagnosed as having tuberculosis. I was quite shattered by the news thinking it was a death sentence and was hospitalised at the Mathilda Hospital on Hong Kong Island. The hospital was situated on the Peak with extensive views overlooking the back way into Hong Kong. It was more than two weeks before I plucked up the courage to ask the doctor how long I had left to live. He laughed and said to a ripe old age if I behaved myself and took the medication prescribed. The relief was quite immense and even after half a century I can still recreate the feeling.

I was there for two months. Captain Parrish, the marine-superintendent, visited me every week, for which courtesy I am eternally grateful. Colin De Mowbray, a lieutenant in the Navy who lived in Lymington – and whose brother was at school with me but was tragically killed in a car crash – visited. He regaled me with stories of his runs ashore in Hong Kong, including a most amusing story of a one-legged lady. Graham turned up quite often and eventually I obtained permission from the company and the doctor to go and stay with him. A married couple lived in, cook and house boy, so I was properly looked after. His flat was at middle level with a grand view over the harbour in front of the airport.

I was eventually declared fit enough to go back to sea but was not allowed any alcohol and was obliged to take 64 pills a day for the next three years.

H BOATS

I joined the "Hang Sang", sister ship to the "Ho Sang", on the Borneo run. The first master was a dour Australian and after him a total nut-case called White. I got on well enough with White by ignoring him!

I was determined to get the record for the most logs carried north-bound, but this was only possible if enough 'sinkers' – the heavy logs – were supplied early in the loading to give stability. The final loading was done by lifting a log and, if the ship heeled too much, put it back in the water and call it a day. I would then work out the stability, making sure we had positive stability going into Hong Kong. On one voyage I made it with the logs stacked high on deck. The only problem occurred in Hong Kong. The ship was, of course, extremely tender; I should think we were lucky if we had zero stability, let alone positive. Captain Parrish stepped onto the gangway at the same time the crew raised and swung out a derrick. The ship listed and Captain Parrish got his feet wet. He was not pleased and read me the riot act about being irresponsible. He later congratulated me on the amount of logs we had carried – a record!

The logs were discharged and we brought the "Hang Sang" round to the harbour for loading. The lowly H boats were not moored to No. 1 buoy but further down the fairway towards Stonecutter Island. There was a typhoon warning out and cargo work stopped, the barges all seeking shelter in the gathering gloom. When it was obvious the typhoon was going to pass over Hong Kong I suggested to Graham Taylor, the new master, that we should veer out more cable to the buoy but he did not agree. It is obvious to the most simple-minded that the shorter the cable the more likely it is to break in bad conditions. The longer the cable the bigger the catenary, the more it sags the less likely it is to part in the gusts if the ship started to snub. I explained, cajoled, persuaded all to no avail.

Maybe I should have slacked out more cable on my own volition but it would have been direct disobedience. I told the master that it was inevitable the cable would break. He did agree to let me drop the anchor under foot. The wind increased during the night to typhoon force and then dropped to nothing as the eye passed over Hong Kong.

"There you are, I told you we would be OK," said Graham smugly during the lull.

How stupid can a person be?

"We have been lucky," I replied. "Now is the time to slack out more cable before the wind is even stronger from the opposite direction."

"No, she will be OK," he countered.

"You're wrong, we are in ballast and we will break loose." I argued but it was to no avail.

The wind increased in a few minutes to typhoon force with even greater intensity than before. We were on the bridge listening to the VHF and ships were beginning to drag their anchors or break adrift. I knew it was only a matter of time before we did the same.

The crew were frightened and Graham ordered everyone to wear their life jackets, which was not exactly a morale booster. The wind howled round the old-fashioned bridge and increased even more to a shriek. The windows of the wheelhouse rattled in their sockets, the glass criss-crossed with tape in case they smashed. The ship started to snub or jerk at the cable as the sea got up even in the shelter of Hong Kong Harbour. The engines were on standby and I suggested that we steam ahead to ease the tension on the cable, but I was shouting at a frightened man and it was to no avail. The inevitable occurred and the cable snapped with a bang clearly audible over the shrieking wind. The "Hang Sang" took off like a rocket down the harbour completely out of control, dragging the anchor I had let go. I crawled forward with the bosun. It was completely impossible to stand up in the wind, and, somehow, we slacked out more cable until almost all of it was out. Why it did not break when the weight came on I do not know, but it did not. I crawled back to the bridge and insisted that we steam slowly ahead to help the cable, which Graham agreed to. We were close to another ship but swinging clear.

As the night drew on so the wind slowly moderated and in the daylight we took stock of our position. The funnel was almost bare, the point stripped off. We had drifted past half a dozen ships and it was a complete miracle we had not hit any. We later shifted back to our buoy, the broken cable hanging in the water. The marine superintendent when he came onboard asked me why I thought we had broken adrift and I told him straight.

HOMEWARD BOUND

I was due leave but there was an emergency and I joined the "Eastern Ranger" as chief officer for the trip up to Japan. On the way we had very bad weather skirting another typhoon, which did not do my nerves much good. I was ready for leave. The tour of duty had been reduced from four years to two and a half. I had served two years and ten months – time off sick did not count – and I had my sea time in to sit for my master's certificate.

I flew down to Hong Kong and tidied up my affairs, including paying Hong Kong income tax. Pan American Airlines was the cheapest way to fly home via the places I wanted to see. I flew to New Delhi and spent the night in the very grand Ashoka Hotel. The next day I flew Royal Nepal Airways over the mountains to Kathmandu. What a contrast for me to be 4,000 feet above sea level and no sea! Unfortunately, the country was in mourning for King Mahendra had died and everything was shut. Luckily the hotel bar man was susceptible to a small honorarium and I could still get a drink in the bar where I met another Englishman, David Lomax, who was doing a television thing.

The next day I hired a car and driver and was driven on the newly-made road to the Tibetan border. The scenery was spectacular, with deep gorges and high mountains. At the border there was a bridge and in the middle was a Chinese guard. I got out of the car and walked up to the bridge. When I stepped up on to it the guard lifted his rifle and as I moved closer to him, he pointed it at me. I considered honour to have been satisfied having stood on the bridge and backed off, the guard lowering his rifle when I was back on the road. I got in the car with driver shaking his head! He did not speak any English.

On my last day the weather was fine and clear. I again hired a car and driver and was driven as far up the nearest mountain as possible. I walked further and enjoyed the most spectacular and awe-inspiring view of the Himalayas stretching into the distance, the peaks all glistening white in the sunlight – the rugged scenery still 'flashes upon the inward eye' – and the silence. It made me feel insignificant amongst such natural majesty, but a truly spiritual experience.

The flight back to New Delhi was bumpy and low cloud hid the view. I took off in a Pan American flight bound west. About ten minutes into the air the captain of the Boeing 707 announced, "We have an electrical fault and when we have jettisoned the fuel we will return to New Delhi."

A short while later I looked out of the window and saw flames shooting out of the starboard inner jet. I almost froze in shock and thought my last moment had come. I pressed the buzzer for the stewardess and when she arrived pointed out the flames. She fairly flew back to a telephone, and in a little while the flames stopped. The jet had been shut down.

We landed at New Delhi with fire engines on the runway. The passengers disembarked onto the runway and were led into the airport building. I was a bag of nerves – the Hang Sang typhoon, skirting the one on the way to Pusan, and now this. I thought I would never make it home.

I accosted a Pan American stewardess and asked how I could be transferred to a BOAC plane I had seen sitting on the runway. She was very good, telling me not to worry, everything was going to be all right and no, I could not transfer.

Some hours later – and no doubt, a modicum of liquid refreshment – we all got on the same plane and it took off for Rome, the electrical fault had been corrected and I was assured the flames I had seen were quite normal when fuel was being jettisoned. I wondered.

Rome was the first European city I stayed in for almost three years. I enjoyed walking the streets admiring the buildings – the Colosseum, St Peter's Cathedral, the Vatican – and eating Italian food. I attended the opera in the imposing Rome Opera House.

While sitting in the upstairs bar of the hotel I was staying at I was called to the telephone and heard my elder brother at the other end urging me to get home to go to the Daffodil Ball, or some such thing. I don't know how he had tracked me down but I cut short my Rome visit and went to the Ball.

ANATINA

It was the summer of 1968. My elder brother Donald worked for Herbert Despard, the founder and chairman of Cannon Street Investments. He was a co-founder of Slater Walker, but had set out on his own and been successful. Arthur Rob died while designing a beautiful sketch, the design drawings being finished by Robert Clark. Herbert had her built in wood and fitted out to be the ultimate cruising machine. Donald supervised the building and introduced me to Herbert. He asked to sail with them to Norway.

"Anatina" was 54 feet long with a long keel and drew 6 feet, with wooden-laid decks, masts and spars. Down below, the cabin was open plan with white settees in the saloon and a wooden-laid cabin sole. The whole effect was light and airy with a feeling of space.

There was a fridge – an unheard of luxury in those days – single side band radio, VHF, and the first Decca Navigator fitted to a yacht. This was before the days of modern electronics and the machine was a big ship one on hire from Decca and required a set of Decca latticed charts.

She was very comfortable to sail and the diesel engine gave a cruising speed of six knots. Herbert and Minda, his wife, always supplied the best of food and wine. It was a marvellous six day passage to Kristiansand on the South coast of Norway. I was the navigator. We then cruised the inner leads to Oslo and back to the island they owned situated inside the outer island of Jomfruland. The nearest town was Kragero reached by speed boat.

We spent some time at the summer house – various guests arriving and leaving – and then sailed to Marstrand in Sweden, cruising back through the inner leads to the island. Herbert was a marvellous skipper and host and the yacht ran like clockwork with a happy atmosphere on board.

I flew home to England and set off with my mother in "Mary

Helen". She was 26 feet overall with no mod cons at all. There was a compass, a hand lead line, and I took my sextant with me. What a contrast to "Anatina"!

MARY HELEN

We sailed down into the Bay of Biscay just south of La Rochelle under the bridge to Ile D'Oleron ending up the canal to Marennes. We were the first British yacht to visit the port since the end of the war and we stayed for three days rent free. A fisherman, Maurice South took me out on his boat fishing in the Coureau d'Oleron starting at 03:00 and by 04:00 we were drinking red wine and eating oysters, bread and cheese. He took me to look at the Pertuis de Maumusson which my mother wished to pass through. We returned about noon having a good day! I told my mother, "There were great breaking seas right across the entrance, and pyramids of solid water leaping into the air. No place for big or small." We did not leave by that passage. We returned to Lymington having visited 41 places in 47 days. She won the Royal Cruising Club Founders Cup for this cruise.

All the gallivanting around on yachts was not advancing my career, least of all obtaining my master's certificate. It was time to go back to work. I went to South Western House in Southampton – the examination centre for masters and mates – to have my sea time checked before going to school. To my complete horror I found I was a month short, and sailing in yachts did not count. I checked with the chief examiner Captain Freaker that a coastal voyage would be sufficient and joined Stephenson and Clark. I travelled to Newcastle and found the small collier "Amberley".

This was something else again – home trade coasting. There was the master, me the mate, a Pakistani second mate and numerous crew. However, only half the crew were apparently on board the ship at any one time, although all on the payroll. When I questioned the philosophy of paying people to do no work, I was told to mind my own business! Which I did.

The master did not keep a watch so it was four hours on and four hours off for the Pakistani and myself. We took a full cargo of coal from Newcastle – all of 2,000 tons – and discharged on a river berth so the "Amberley" took the ground at low tide.

We steamed in ballast to Rotterdam, cleaning the holds on the way for a full cargo of grain to Middlesbrough. My month was up and I packed my bags and left, wondering how on earth the company made any money. It had been an interesting experience but not one I wished to repeat! The Amberley was lost in a storm 1973. "Anatina" was much more fun.

MASTERS

I went to the School of Navigation at Warsash, as I had done for my other certificates, and studied hard. The South Africans were lively people so I tended to mix with them, boozing in the Silver Fern after an evening's study.

I lived at the school, taking my meals in the dining-room with its magnificent view over Southampton Water. England was very different from Hong Kong and seemed to be peopled by people who were different from the English in Hong Kong. Maybe it was because everyone worked in Hong Kong there were no hand outs.

It was the first Christmas I spent at home since going to sea, which was fun. My first Christmas away was on the "Dara" in Bombay; "Okla" in Cochin; "Bulimba" in Chalna; "City of Oxford" at sea; "City of Worcester" in Chalna; "Eastern Star" in Sydney; "Eastern Maid" in Calcutta.

I failed the written examination on my first attempt; although I passed the individual exams I did not reach the overall 70 per cent pass mark required. I passed on my next attempt, and orals. I was given my 'coveted' pink slip, but they would not give me my certificate until my 26th birthday, I was too young. I was quite satisfied with myself, having achieved an objective – my master's. I wrote to Indo China to tell them the good news and they wrote back to inform me I was redundant, which pricked my little bubble! It was spring 1969.

MY FIRST COMMAND

I heard of someone wanting a master for a delivery voyage. I met the owner or organiser, I am not sure which, and ended up as master of a tug and three tows. The tug was lying in Portsmouth and not in her first youth, so I recruited a retired engineer commander through an R.N. friend as the chief engineer to keep her going. The four tugs had been sold to Italy, the three tows to be dropped off at Naples and the towing tug at Ancona. I knew nothing about towing but learnt quickly.

The crew were an assortment but someone must have known what they were doing because the tows were rigged, approved for insurance, and I set off with my first command before the age of 26! The tows were alongside until outside the harbour and the pilot had disembarked. We streamed them successfully one behind the other and set off down channel in fine weather and across the Bay of Biscay.

"We're sinking!" the anguished voice of the chief engineer shouted as he ran onto the bridge.

It was a fine sunny day and I had just taken the morning sight. My heart stopped and I projected forward to the Court of Enquiry taking away my not yet issued certificate.

I calmed Jack down enough to discover that water was coming into the engine room bilges. We quickly investigated and I discovered that the water – which was salt, so sea water – was coming from above the apparent waterline and was not continuous.

"The pumps are containing it!" I shouted over the roar of the engine.

"Yes," he replied, giving the thumbs up signal.

"Let's go on deck and take a look."

We went out of the engine room and onto the tow deck, keeping below the tow wire. I looked over the side at the approximate place we had seen the water and saw a scupper hole. Water was slopping onto the deck as the tug rolled in the swell, but not coming out of the scupper hole – the pipe was broken. It was a matter of minutes to plug the scupper and the hull was tight again.

There were no other incidents and I successfully dropped off the three smaller tows at Naples. We had a pleasant free run round to Ancona. No one answered the VHF when I arrived outside the harbour, so I steamed inside and blew the whistle. It was remarkable how quickly a pilot and various officials turned up! I berthed her alongside the quay and the new owner gave the chief and I a very good lunch sitting in the sun.

ANATINA

Back in England Donald was fitting out "Anatina", and Herbert asked me to join them for the summer cruise. It was to be a little more ambitious and as navigator I had fun ordering the charts. I like British Admiralty charts; I like looking at them and planning where I would like to go, whether a fascinating looking cove is a suitable anchorage or not.

Herbert, Donald and I set off together with various of Herbert's friends for Norway and the summer house on the island. The weather was not very good and we were glad to make Kristiansand. Various cruises were made along the coast, "Anatina" being much admired wherever she went.

Later in the summer we sailed across the North Sea in very bad weather. The yacht behaved well in the gale force conditions. Luckily the wind was astern but it was very rough.

We called in at a fishing port unused to yachts to repair the decca. Then on up the Firth in the rain to Inverness. The Caledonian Canal is very beautiful, even in the rain. We sailed from Fort William to Mallaig, and then into a cove behind Loch Morar where Herbert had laid a mooring. He owned Morar Estate – some 10,000 acres of hill – with a lodge on Loch Morar. The scenery was spectacular, with the heather turning, and it was very peaceful. A fast landing craft was used to transport people and stores up the loch to Mallaig. It was a stalking estate, which was not my scene, but it was great to walk and fish.

My father travelled north and joined us for the sail south. It was late in the year and it was a matter of dodging the gales as best we could. It was just the three of us on board – Donald, my father and myself. We were storm bound in Holyhead some days, even laying out the fisherman's anchor to prevent "Anatina" from dragging.

A young lady swam out to the yacht one day and I fell in love! She was staying at the Fishguard Hotel and we dined there when we could get ashore. We left between gales and got round the Lizard before the next one hit. We raced up the channel at ten knots, surfing on the waves, just missing the RCC meet which we wanted to attend in the Beaulieu River. "Anatina", with her long keel, was very comfortable in the rough weather.

I corresponded frequently with my American lady friend from Fishguard, but we did not meet again for some time. After a summer sailing it was time to get on with my career – the next objective being to obtain command as quickly as possible. I had no desire to be at sea for the next 35 years, but I did want a command before coming ashore. Indo China was an excellent company to work for, with good promotion, a non-contributory pension and retirement after 20 years' service. If I had not been made redundant I would have retired at 43 years of age! However, I had been made redundant – no doubt being ill twice had not helped – so I knew I had t find another company. I picked Bank Line because I thought promotion would be quick.

BANK LINE

I went for an interview at the offices of Andrew Weir, the owner of Bank Line, and was offered a job as chief officer on one of their new ships the "Teviotbank". I joined her in Antwerp where she was loading urea for Chittagong.

Well, I did not know quite what to expect but I did not know that people like Captain Howe existed, I thought they were figments of rather twisted imaginations. He was a loud-mouthed martinet from the previous century, and the only saving grace was that his wife was on board. I knew I was in for trouble within minutes of walking on board. The chief officer I relieved could not get off the ship quick enough, and Captain Howe was shouting almost as soon as I met him. I almost walked off the ship then and there before signing on. However, I made an inspection of the ship and liked what I saw so decided to 'give it a go' and try to find some sort of accommodation with the master.

The chief engineer was an elderly man and I commiserated with him. When Howe goaded me too far I lost my temper and was about to attack him outside my cabin. The chief prevented it by placing himself between us. I am exceedingly grateful to him, for attacking a British master on his own ship is a very serious offence indeed – especially for a chief officer. However, it had its effect and Howe toned himself down after that incident.

We discharged the fertiliser at Chittagong, where I did not go ashore. In ballast it was normal for the deep tanks to be ballasted to give the ship some draft. However, Howe wanted the deep tanks cleaned and would not listen to reason – either from me or the chief engineer.

We went to Trincomalee completely light, with the foot of the bow almost out of the water. The pilot came on board and remonstrated with Captain Howe, telling him he would not berth the ship until there was some ballast in her. At least I was vindicated. We carried on to Visakhapatnam, where we loaded a full cargo of iron ore for Japan. The agent took me out for a couple of good curries.

While getting the ropes out of the hold prior to arrival in Japan, I squashed the third finger on my right hand. It was incredibly painful, with part of the nail ripped off. Once in port I went to the hospital where, watched by a couple of smiling nurses, the doctor started to remove the rest of the nail. The pain was quite excruciating but I was determined not to cry out in front of the still smiling nurses. I asked for an anaesthetic. I got it – two injections into the open nail bed, which was almost as painful as having my finger nail removed without it. Once the bits were taken out, he stitched up the mess and I returned to the ship. The finger was painful for weeks and the stitches were removed, painfully, in Glasgow.

After the discharge in Japan, we sailed with the deep tanks full for Australia, where we loaded a full cargo of grain for Scotland. It was the first time I had loaded grain in a tween decker, and the use of feeders was interesting. These were wooden boxes constructed in the tween deck and filled with grain, which kept the grain tight as it settled during the voyage. If the grain was slack it acted rather like water and the ship could end up with negative stability and turn over. Howe ran around like a mad thing but everyone ignored him, the Australian stevedore is a tough nut.

The ship called at Durban for bunkers and I was glad to leave her in Glasgow. The company offered me another new ship but I said that Howe had been enough and left amicably.

I went to London and stayed with my American lady friend. We thought we were in love with one another and decided to make a trip to Bronte country. She was a writer and literary minded. When she came to stay at Thorns Beach my mother put her in the Windmill, which was a good 100 yards from the main house so we were in separate rooms! My parents were a little wary of an American.

I borrowed Edward's blue MGB sports car and we drove to Howarth. The first few days were great, driving round the countryside in a sports car viewing the sights, dining and wining by candlelight, and making love. I thought this is it. She asked me to marry her and I demurred at first and then things changed. What had been an idyllic pre honeymoon love affair turned into a disaster. I cut short the trip and drove her back to London in stony silence. I have not seen or heard of her from that day to this. What went wrong I still don't know, but it took a long time for the emotional wounds to heal.

ANATINA

The summer was coming up, "Anatina" was ready to sail, and I was asked to navigate. I had fun buying the charts for this summer's cruise. Herbert, Donald and I set off from Lymington, west about round Land's End and up the Irish Sea to Scotland. At Mallaig we bunkered and carried on north through the beautiful Western Isles past Skye to Stornoway, which we entered at night on the radar.

The next day we set sail out into the Atlantic, with a good forecast. A few days later the weather changed, the barometer started falling and we knew we were in for a blow whatever the forecast said. The wind increased and we reefed. The wind increased more and we took in more reefs until, finally, we lowered the mainsail completely. It was already difficult to carry on a conversation in the cockpit with the wind howling in the rigging, the air filled with spume off the sea, and the waves beginning to break.

The barometer fell even further and the wind increased to storm force 10. We lowered the mizzen and staysail and lay a hull. It was daylight but the visibility was restricted by tops of the waves being blown off, filling the air with spume. "Anatina" lay very comfortably about 60 degrees off, the wind lifting to the sea. An occasional breaking crest came on board but nothing serious.

The storm shutters were put on the dog house windows. Down below the fruit bowl remained on the table, which had the fiddles up. Meals were eaten in their usual style with a glass of wine. Every ten minutes or so the man on watch would have a look on deck to see that all was well and there were no ships, not that we were in an exactly crowded part of the ocean.

The barometer fell to 954 millibars, which is very low indeed for summer, and the anemometer blew off the top of the mast in a gust of perhaps force 11. Donald, when sailing with Lord Riverdale, had experienced similar weather but "Bluebird" was in the Gulf stream off the American coast and the seas were much worse. They had been forced to run before it. We certainly did not wish to run because that would have taken us away from our destination and "Anatina" was riding the weather exceptionally well.

We chatted about life and this and that because it is not every day one is out in a small yacht in storm conditions north of Scotland, not far from the Arctic Circle!

When the wind fell to about force 9 we hoisted a small bit of the mizzen to keep the bow up towards the wind.

The next day the weather moderated enough to make sail and we resumed our course.

"What is that glinting in the sunlight to starboard?" asked Donald.

We could not make it out, looked at the chart and then realised that it was from the four glaciers on the Southern mainland of Iceland. It was a stirring sight. Heimaey was sighted ahead and we headed towards the harbour, which meant steering straight at the vertical cliff and then, at the last moment, altering course to port and passing through the narrow entrance. Some years later the entrance was closed by a lava flow during an eruption of the volcano whose crater lies above the town.

We were very pleased with ourselves to have made Iceland, Herbert's white ensign causing nothing more than curiosity. We celebrated no more than usual, well, maybe an extra bottle of champagne!

We climbed up the black grit to the crater above the town. A few days later we sailed on to Reykjavik. The Cod War was on but again, even though the gunboats were in port, no one took any notice of the white ensign, except idle curiosity.

Herbert hired a car and we drove around the lunar-looking landscape along un-metalled roads. Once we were stopped by the police for speeding and promised to be good. It was completely different from anything I had seen elsewhere.

Herbert went home for Minda's birthday and Malcolm, our fourth brother, turned up. We flew up to Akureyri spending most of the flight in the cockpit, including landing. This was north of the Arctic Circle. We took a tour and swam in hot springs, admiring the rugged scenery.

When Herbert returned we sailed to Horndafjordur, passing the new volcanic island of Surtsey which only appeared in 1963 after a volcanic eruption. We were probably the first British yacht to pass it. Some fishermen came on board and gave us a fresh halibut, which was quite delicious with red wine.

We continued along the spectacular South coast of Iceland and made a passage to the Faeroe Islands. My mother visited the Faeroes when she was 17 with her father in his un-engined yacht "Emmanuel" and published an account *Adventures in the Faeroes*.

Malcolm did not really like the passages, being seasick, but he kept his watch. Bergen was the next stop and it rained, in sharp contrast to the heatwave we had in Iceland. Malcolm flew home and Minda joined, along with other guests.

We mainly motored through the inner leads in rain to the Sognefjord where we celebrated midsummer's day – a most important day for Norwegians. Various crew, sometimes just Donald and I, took the yacht back through the inner leads to the island. The Norwegian scenery in the inner leads was fascinating, originally marked for sailing ships with ring bolts in places so they could warp the ship. The view was always changing from rugged rocks to hills and mountains, passing through gaily painted, wooden house villages.

INDO CHINA AGAIN

I flew home and rejoined Indo China Steam Navigation Company Limited. The company had a joint venture deal with Divlov Simmerson, a Norwegian company, whereby Indo China manned and managed the ship. I am not sure who the owner was but the deal was to unlock subsidies from governments to build ships.

I travelled by ferry to Denmark, train to Copenhagen and ferry to Landskrona where the "Vianna" was being built. She was an ore oil bulk carrier of some 100,000 tons, a far cry from the traditional Indo China ship – but the world of shipping was changing. Ship building is not my forte although quite interesting.

I was designated to take over as chief officer once I had learnt the ropes because I had never been on a tanker. The important thing was to learn the piping system and how to load and discharge oil cargo. Frankly, it left me stone cold but I buckled down and pretended enthusiasm. Buller Cole was the master and had never been on a tanker either. The chief officer was the only one with tanker experience, so he had to teach us all. It was in his interest to make sure we learned so he could get off and go on leave.

Landskrona was a small Swedish town, with the shipyard being the main employer. There was no work at the weekends and the town was not exactly a swinging city. However, Copenhagen was only a couple of hours away by ferry and was certainly swinging – I saw my first erotic show with Europeans performing! There is a lot to do, museums to see, the Tivoli Gardens, excellent restaurants and all the attractions of a beautiful capital city.

Edward, who was in the army, was stationed at Osnabruck and I travelled by train from Copenhagen to see him and stay in the officers' mess. It was fun and interesting for me. We arranged to meet at noon on a following Saturday at Hamburg

Railway Station and had a night out on the Ripa Barn, which was 'educational'. On the train back through Germany I pulled out a *Times* to read and the only other occupant of the carriage left. The interesting thing travelling by train was the train ferries between the islands. There was a regular weekend ferry trip to Travemunde in East Germany, which was fun. Most people did not bother to get off in East Germany, the main attraction of the ferry was booze and the facilities on board. It made a very pleasant couple of days' excursion.

The ship was finally completed, sea trials successfully completed, and we sailed in ballast for Ain Sokhna in Egypt, a terminal fifty miles south of Suez. The Suez canal was closed so we rounded Africa picking up mail and stories at Cape town. Loading was completed in 24 hours, a very intensive time for me learning the ropes, and we sailed for Rio de Janeiro again calling at Capetown for mail and stores. The statue of Christ with arms outstretched dominated the skyline at Rio, but there was no time to go ashore. Enterprising Ladies of the Night turned up at the discharge buoy for those who had enough time to so indulge. They had been flown out in helicopters.

We were off within twenty-four hours of arriving, bound for the Persian Gulf in ballast via Capetown where the agent brought out the mail and stores in a launch. We encountered rough weather crossing the South Atlantic and the ship flexed alarmingly, the middle of the ship going up and down some feet.

You are not allowed ashore in Ras Tanura, Saudi Arabia, even if you wanted to and had enough time. The voyage to Japan was uneventful and we discharged at a buoy off Yokohama. Poor old Lee Emery was left as chief officer while I went ashore with Captain Parrish, bound for Hong Kong and the Australian run. Earlier in the voyage I wrote to the office saying that tankers were not for me and requested a transfer. Some time later Lee Emery got his revenge because he ended up with the shore job I was after.

The "Eastern Rover" 4,408 gross tons was a slightly larger cargo ship than the old "Eastern Maid" 3,603 tons and together with the "Eastern Ranger", ran a monthly round trip service from Hong Kong to Brisbane; Sydney; Melbourne; Hobart in Tasmania; Sydney; sometimes Newcastle; Brisbane; Cebu and Manila in the Philippines; Kaohsiung and Keelung in Taiwan; and back to Hong Kong. The success on this run, with its tight schedule, was to load and discharge simultaneously. For instance, in Hong Kong one loaded for all the ports while discharging cargo loaded for Hong Kong at the other ports. It required considerable skill on the part of the chief officer to achieve this without overloading or over-carrying and was a challenge. The occasional Australian strike threw the schedule out with consequent problems for the cargo work. The ship was run in the usual Jardine style and was a lot more fun than tankers. I got on well with George Taylor, the captain, who was very social and had lots of friends around the Australian coast. I saw some Stawell cousins in Hobart and time passed very pleasantly.

All good things come to an end and I flew home for some leave and then joined the "Eastern Saga" in Antwerp. She was a dry bulk carrier. Buller Cole was the master and Don B was the chief engineer. I did a day trip with Don to see the beautiful city of Brussels. We loaded a steel cargo for Houston, Texas.

The "Eastern Saga" was a bulk carrier of 40,000 tons, five hatches served by cranes. It was another joint venture this time with Wah Kwong, a Hong Kong Chinese owned company.

In Houston I hired a car, played golf and saw as much as I could of the States, it being my first visit. We loaded urea in Pascagoula, Alabama, and Baton Rouge up the Mississippi, enabling us to visit New Orleans courtesy of the charterers. We spent all night in the bars listening to jazz and ended up in Tiffany's for a champagne breakfast.

Anchored outside Chittagong lightening ship was a salutary change but the weather was good. The discharge of the free fertiliser for Bangladesh was completed alongside, but Chittagong was not Calcutta.

We sailed in ballast to Bangkok to load a full cargo of manioc for Europe. Both Buller and I had written to the office moaning and groaning about the new ship despite Don's catch phrase, 'If you can't take a joke you shouldn't come to sea!'

I received a letter from David Newbigging, the chairman, explaining how the old Indo China was being grafted onto the new Wah Kwong. The real thing was that I did not like the lowering of standards, nor did Buller. The manager of Jardine Agency took us out and tried to persuade us to stay but it was to no avail. I remained with the ship to Rotterdam, where Donald turned up with a car to take me home with my luggage. I quit smoking. And so finally ended my time with Indo China, one of the oldest British shipping companies founded in 1832 to trade between India and China. They had some of the finest clippers of their day and, with the advent of steam, traded all round the China coast and up the Yangtze. Their forays into tramp shipping as the traditional liner trades folded up ultimately failed and Indo China is no more being liquidated in 1974.

SHORE JOB

This was to be my last year sailing on "Anatina". Herbert, Donald and I left Lymington and had a fast passage across the Bay of Biscay. Bright sunshine and a fair wind down the Portuguese coast soon had us in Lisbon sampling fresh sardines and drinking vinho verde the light white wine. Herbert hired a car and we saw the sights and dined at the best restaurants.

During the trip Herbert and I had chatted away, usually at night. I explained that I had left Indo China and why, and was wondering what to do. He said that he had a lawyer friend who was looking for a master mariner to join his firm. I expressed interest. Herbert phoned Robert Elbourne and I flew to London for an interview held in the City Club. I accepted the job offer and flew back to Lisbon after a good lunch in the Club.

Herbert flew home and Edward joined Donald and me. We made a good passage to the Azores. On the way Donald had done something to the pump. When pumping the bilges one day they started to fill. No one could understand that the faster we pumped the faster the water came in, I really thought we were going to sink. However, when we stopped pumping the level remained the same. Once the valve was turned round all was well, but it gave us all quite a turn!

The Azores were very pleasant; Edward went off and Herbert returned. We motored a good deal of the way to Falmouth, where we bunkered and carried on to Kristiansand. I flew home to London and a new job, and a new way of life with Elbourne Mitchel.

Being a junior legal assistant as opposed to chief officer – with all the domestics taken care of – was a big jump. I had to organise washing my own clothes, shopping for food, and cooking. I gave up and ate out. And I had an hour's commute each way in the underground, which I hated. I hired a room in a mews flat owned by Gilian Green, whom I had met on "Anatina".

I liked the work. Robert Elbourne, ebullient and confident, was senior partner and I worked for him to start with. The firm specialised in marine work and had all sorts of interesting maritime clients.

Robert stalked the floor at Lloyds for work. Stephen Mitchell was the other senior partner but I never really got to know him. Dennis Rixon was the whizz kid at taking evidence on all marine matters: collisions; salvage; fires; and any sort of maritime perils. I got to know him only too well. Ray Clarke worked with Whitehouse Vaux in a separate office and they worked for the Indonesians. Rob Wallis was a laid back, golf-playing articled clerk; while nervous, harassed Keith Barnes did all the back up work for Rixon. Nicholas Burke specialised in charter party work, while Richard Shaw did marine work.

The carpeted offices were at Three Quays on the top floor, with a view overlooking HMS *Belfast*. I was luckily given an office overlooking the river and used to watch what little river traffic there was, sometimes dreaming of the tropics when the rain was pouring down on a winter's day. There was a distinctly daggy pub across the road where we sometimes congregated. Lunch was often eaten in El Corvinos, an expensive underground restaurant close by.

I learnt the ropes by being involved with the cases. Eventually I ended up nominally working for Richard Shaw, but spent a good deal of my time with Dennis Rixon – unfortunately, a lot of it in the pub.

The first case I was sent off on my own on was the salvage of the Woolwich ferry by a Brathwaite and Dean tug. Private submission to arbitration was agreed and I prepared the papers, having taken photographs of the area which enhanced our case. Mr Braithwaite was not unhappy with the result.

A much more difficult case involved a boatyard dispute in Devon. I stayed in a hotel in Torquay and interviewed our client in his house. Another case in Devon involved the salvage of a fishing boat – we acted for the insurer.

I travelled up to Middlesbrough with Rob Wallis for a collision. Our clients were the Poles. Dennis Rixon was nominally in charge but he stayed in London. After taking evidence for about six hours I had a conference with Rob and we realised that the case did not add up. In a flash of understanding I realised that, for the collision to have occurred at all, our ship must have been making stern way. We sat down and retook all the evidence. The one thing I learned was that if you have not got the truth from your client, however bad, you have no case.

On another case we travelled up to Felixstowe where a container ship had knocked a container crane into the water. One of Richard Shaw's cases involved a collision in the river on the way to Antwerp. I prepared the detailed chart from the evidence of the collision for the trial. It was most interesting to attend the court and listen to the evidence and questioning or interrogation of the witnesses. Little did I think I would end up in the court myself one day accused of misrepresentation!

Elborne Mitchell acted for Selco Salvage in Singapore. Robert Elborne was the partner in charge but Dennis Rixon did the work and serviced the client. He considered Selco to be his pet baby and jealously guarded his patch. Keith did the donkey work. Dennis spent a considerable time in Singapore but was in London for most of the arbitrations. I used to attend some of them with him and Keith. I became very interested in salvage, eventually coming to the conclusion that it would be fun to be a salvor.

Dennis Rixon was not an easy person to work with and sometimes was just downright unpleasant, so unpleasant that I did not want to work with him. He could be charming when he wanted to impress.

I often worked late in the office when Dennis was in town, sending telexes for him – mainly to Singapore. The time difference meant that Singapore opened just as London was closing. After 18:00 in the office there was normally a bottle of wine to keep us going. A walk across the street into the daggy pub for the final one for the road often meant I did not get back to the mews flat until 21:00, much too late to start cooking. Dennis must have arrived home in Bromley even later, which could not have been much fun for his wife.

I went home most weekends to Thorns Beach and was glad to get out of London, but I hated the return on Sunday night. I could have had a much more active social life but funds were tight and, at the age of 30, it was embarrassing.

I sailed with different new friends on some weekends in the summer of 1973, once driving down to Hamble with a young barrister in his Bristol.

Donald lived in London in the winter and I sometimes met him in the Royal Ocean Racing Club rooms in St James. One evening I met Norvella and I fell in love. Donald departed and I had dinner with her in her flat in Westminster. We saw a lot of each other and I asked her to marry me but she said, "You are too immature, come back in a couple of years' time."

About a year after joining the firm, Alan Bond, the Selco manager, was in London and I arranged to have an interview with him during a weekend. Herbert Despard lent me his Volvo. I drove to Dungeness and found the pub where I met Mr Bond, a tall taciturn man. To this day I do not know why the pub at Dungeness was chosen for the interview because Bond was staying in London. He drove down in a chartered Ferrari. I was duly interviewed and offered a job as chief officer on the new tug Selco had bought in Japan. I accepted. Dennis Rixon was not the only reason for wanting to leave London. My salary was derisory compared to that of chief officer and I was living on my savings, but these had gone up the spout with some disastrous stock exchange investments. In fact, I owed a lot of money to the bank.

I must have fallen out with Gilian because the last month I spent in London was on my credit card, living in a hotel in Green Park, increasing my debt to the bank. It was with mixed feelings I left London. Robert Elbourne had been very good to me and encouraged me to become qualified while Dennis Rixon was dead against it. I realised later that he considered me a threat to his position and was glad to get rid of me.

I flew off to Singapore and a completely new life.

NEW LIFE SALVAGE. SALVALIANT

I arrived in Singapore during the summer of 1974 and it was hot and humid. I was put up at the Orchid Inn on the Bukit Timah Road. I arrived at the office out at Jurong – about forty-five minutes' drive from the hotel – wearing a tie and jacket. I soon realised my mistake.

No one seemed very interested in me so I wandered around the shipyard for, apart from tugs and barges, Selco owned a yard and slip. Tony Church, an ex-seafarer, took pity on me and lent me a car for a couple of weeks to drive around and 'learn' Singapore. Being the marketing man he always wore a tie but no jacket. Eventually I was given small jobs to do including sea trials of two small tugs the yard built which was interesting.

Captain Peter Lankester arrived with the 'new' tug. She was an old Japanese tug driven by two engines coupled to a single shaft. Manoeuvring was done on one engine and to stop the propeller, the engine had to be stopped, big ship style. The "Daisy," 993 gross tons, length 186 feet, and draught 15 feet, powered by two Burmeister & Wain engines totalling 4,600 indicated horse power giving a speed of 15 knots. was to be completely refitted at Selco Shipyard. Peter, being a most experienced tug master, knew exactly what he wanted done – regardless of expense. She was renamed "Salvaliant." The refit was to take months and I lived in the hotel, going to the tug each day with Peter.

Peter Lankester was a big, heavy, burly, tough Dutchman with a heart of gold. It was hot in Singapore – being almost on the equator – so lunch was normally at the swimming club, accompanied by a few beers to replace all the sweat lost during the morning! The same in the evening on the way back to the hotel.

Peter lived in a flat on the other side of the city with his wife, Unke, and their two children, Peter and Caroline. At weekends I would sometimes go for barbecues.

Knobby Halls, a retired naval petty officer, was the engineer-superintendent. In fact, he doubled as marine-superintendent as well. He was a down-to-earth capable man who got things done and was enormously helpful and supportive to me. He and his wife, Anne, lived in a flat at Sembawang, the naval base, and when I got to know Knobby better I used to go and stay for a night away from the tug.

Ernie Kahlenberg, an older man, was the live wire – the dynamo of Selco – and he seemed to take a shine to me asking me out for Sunday lunch and to visit his house to meet his wife, He used to arrive at the office in a big chauffeur-driven car; a diminutive little man sitting in the back – his white, rather sparse, hair just visible through the back window. He was the chairman and managing director and owned the company.

One evening I received a call from Selco's operation room. We were all on pagers when away from the office or tugs. A van would pick me up and take me to the office. In the operations room I was instructed to go with the "Salvana" and her Filipino master, Captain Hannibal, and tow in a ship from the Malacca Straits.

The "Salvana" was the original 'big' Selco tug of some 2,500 HP and Peter had been in command. This was my first job and I was very excited. The "Salvana" was in the shipyard and it was near low tide so required a small tug to tow her out. We did not want any damage to the propeller. Once clear of the yard Captain Hannibal, having obtained permission from port control, steamed west at full speed through Western Anchorage and into the Malacca Straits. In Singapore no one moved in the port without permission unless they wanted a one-way trip to Changi jail. Any other salvage tug in Singapore would be monitoring the VHF and know that a Selco tug had sailed. What they would not know was whether it was a salvage sailing or not.

The sea was calm in the Malacca Straits – Indonesia to port, Malaysia to starboard – and it was a fine night. There was the usual traffic in the straits, the main gateway to Japan: laden tankers from the Persian Gulf; container ships from Europe; and small fishing boats from both sides. The tug seemed very small compared to the ships I had been on but her 12 knots seemed much faster being so close to the water.

I did not like to admit to Captain Hannibal – a very experienced salvage tug master – that I had no salvage experience although I had towed the minesweepers to Italy. I suspect he knew in any event because there was a pretty good bush telegraph in Selco, especially amongst the Filipinos.

I went onto the tow deck to watch the crew preparing the towing gear. The 'casualty', as a ship in distress is known in the salvage world, was anchored about forty miles north of Singapore. It was about 02:00 in the morning when we reached her. Operations had given me the position.

Captain Hannibal stood by the anchored ship while I went across in the rubber boat. A wooden pilot ladder was lowered and I climbed on board with a Lloyd's Open Form in my pocket. I was taken to the bridge and met the master, a Korean. I offered him the form. He knew we were coming and agreed to sign. I filled it in and we both signed. I was immensely pleased, it was my first Lloyd's Form – the no cure, no pay contract that salvors work on.

I called up the "Salvana" on the portable VHF with Selco's private frequency.

"LOF signed. You can come alongside and connect up, Captain," I spoke into the radio. "Inform Ops."

"Roger, Cap," came the reply through the speaker. Captain Hannibal did not waste words.

The casualty was stemming the tide, that is bow to the tide. In order to make the connection easily and quickly it was necessary for Captain Hannibal to bring the "Salvana" alongside in the 69 position, that is the stern of the tug to the bow of the casualty. He had to come alongside with the tide behind him – not an easy manoeuvre with a single screw tug – and, to stop the propeller turning, the engine had to be stopped. Captain Hannibal did it very well with the crew of the casualty taking the lines. The "Salvana" crew soon had the towing gear connected up. I instructed the master of the casualty to heave up his anchor and remained forward with the two "Salvana" riding crew.

"Anchor is aweigh," I told Captain Hannibal on the radio. "Take her away."

"Let go the tug lines," I instructed the riding crew.

When the lines were pulled in the "Salvana" manoeuvered clear of the casualty, turning to starboard and steaming ahead to commence the tow. When I saw the towing gear was all in order I went to the bridge and remained there with the master. The riding crew greased the fairlead at regular intervals to protect the tow wire. The ship followed the tug very well.

At the pilot station Captain Hannibal anchored the "Salvana" while the Immigration and Customs formalities were completed and with a pilot on board, picked up the anchor and proceeded the short distance in to Western Anchorage.

I was on the forecastle of the casualty when the towing gear was slipped and the anchor let go. The master signed the termination letter and I returned to the "Salvana" in the rubber boat. The sun seemed to be shining particularly brightly.

Captain Hannibal took the "Salvana" back to the yard where – very pleased with myself – I took the LOF to Ops, only to be told that Chris Herbert had agreed a contract tow. So much for my first LOF and salvage bonus. And I had kept such good notes as well!

The "Salvaliant", ex "Daisy", was moored alongside the yard; all sorts of shipyard gear on deck – pipe, bits of metal, all the usual chaos of a ship under refit. Peter received the word that there was a ship aground on Nipa Shoal and the "Salvaliant" was needed.

"Hoffre Domma!" he exclaimed. "How do they expect us to get this heap of garbage away, look at all the junk on deck."

But within the hour the "Salvaliant" was under way to Nipa Shoal. The Shoal is just inside Indonesian waters with a light maintained by the Indonesians, which meant it was out as often as it was lit. Nipa Shoal was christened 'Selco treasure island' because of the number of ships Selco salved there.

The crew and I worked like mad things to get the towing deck and gear ready. We were almost ready by the time we reached Nipa, about an hour's steaming from the yard. I unfortunately badly twisted my ankle on one of the pipes on the tow deck so strapped it up and wore a pair of boots. It was three months before I could take the bandage off, but it did not stop me working – it was much too exciting. Peter just told me to be more careful in future and handed me a cold beer.

The "Frederich Engels", a modern East German cargo ship of some 11,000 gross tons, was almost high and dry on the reef. She was in ballast and had gone aground at full speed believed to have been 22 knots. Peter anchored the "Salvaliant" close by and sent me across in the rubber boat to find out what was going on. I found Captain Hancox, the salvage master, with the captain of the ship. Captain Hancox was a thin, dour individual who was for ever writing – filling his note book in neat black print. He spoke in a one tone Australian voice. Peter did not care for him which was why I had been sent across. Captain Hancox told me that the LOF was signed and the "Salvaliant" should be connected as quickly as possible.

I was elated and was back on the "Salvaliant" as quickly as possible. Good portable radios were expensive and heavy in those days and Selco only had a limited number. We were pretty sure our main rivals listened in to our private frequency so, until a salvage contract was signed, the radios were used as little as possible.

"Hoffre Domma!" exclaimed Peter on the bridge of the tug, opening a cold can of beer and passing me one.

It was hot and the sun was shining brightly. He proceeded to explain how he intended to connect. I was to sound round the stern of the casualty, which was still in the water. He would anchor the "Salvaliant" as close as possible, send away a messenger attached to a mooring line attached to the towing gear, and I would heave it in on board the grounded ship using the capstan. The pelican hook – a huge, quick release hook – and its wire strop would be taken across to the casualty in the rubber boat and I would heave it up on deck using the ship's capstan aft. I would make it fast round one set of bitts and back it up to another set of bitts. When the eye of the towing gear was on deck it would be connected to the pelican hook.

This was all done within an hour or so and the "Salvaliant" was connected. The crew worked really well under the bosun Javier Patani. The towing gear was paid out. It consisted of a 60 foot wire strop of 8 inch circumference wire connected to a 50 foot double nylon stretcher, the nylon being 12 inch circumference. This was connected to the main tow wire, which was 2,000 feet of 6 inch circumference wire on an electrically driven drum which enabled it to be heaved in or slacked out as required.

The anchor on the "Salvaliant" was heaved up and Peter manoeuvred the tug astern of the casualty while the main tow wire was paid out. He then re-anchored to await Captain Hancox's instructions.

I was sent back on board the "Frederich Engels" to see Captain Hancox. He was very informative, told me the fuel and ballast situation and the results of the diving survey.

"Even after all the fuel, water and ballast have been taken off, my calculations suggest the ground reaction is still over 2,000 tons. We will have to cut her up."

He drawled in his usual monotone and Australian accent with a deadpan serious face. It was some time before I realised it was supposed to be a joke, most unusual for him I learned over time.

"It will be high water in an hour and we will have a go with the "Salvaliant" to show willing, but it will be a complete waste of time. Keep the salvage association surveyor happy," he continued, "tell Peter to heave up his anchor and start towing. I will keep in touch on the Selco network."

I returned to the tug and gave him Captain Hancox's instructions.

"Hoffre Domma!" exploded Peter, handing me a cold beer as he flipped open one for himself. "What does that idiot think he is doing, that thing won't come off in a hundred years!"

The anchor was heaved up and Peter showed and taught me his skill as a tug man, explaining everything he did. There was a slight cross current so he had to angle the tug with the tow line out on one side to keep the tug on course. He turned the tug each way to get the feel of her because she was a lot bigger than the "Salvana", and at that moment we were only on half power.

"I don't want to talk to that idiot, so you man the radio," Peter instructed me.

I informed Captain Hancox of the situation and he told me to build up to full power. The manoeuvring position on the monkey island was yet to be fitted, so Peter shouted the engine movements he wanted to me from on top of the bridge where he could see the tow wire.

I rang down to the engine room and told them to start up the second engine. When the engine was clutched onto the shaft, the surge of power could be seen as the tow wire almost came out of the water. Peter explained that the skill was to have enough tow wire out so that it did not break when full power was applied, but not too much so that it dragged along the bottom and damaged itself on the coral.

When the engines were on full power I informed Captain Hancox on the radio.

"Throw her about a bit," I relayed to Peter.

He came down onto the bridge and shouted helm instructions from the bridge wing. The wheel was put hard a starboard and the tug turned to starboard into the current, heeling as she moved sideways through the water. The tow wire came out of the water as the weight of the tug was added to the engine power. Then, when close to shallow water, the wheel was put hard a port, the tug turned, heeled and started moving to port sideways through the water, with the current. Peter turned back well before the shallows on this side so the current did not sweep the tug onto the reef as well. The sea was smooth but, even so, the tug heeled so much that water came onto the tow deck each time.

"The tide has started to fall on my marker on the reef, and there is no sign of any movement," Captain Hancox's voice came over the radio. "Cease towing and anchor for the night," he instructed.

Peter heard the radio, put the engine telegraph to half speed, and rang down to tell the engineers to go on one engine.

Shortly afterwards I let go the anchor and paid out enough chain so the "Salvaliant" lay to the tide with the tow wire over the side.

"We will keep anchor watches," said Peter, "if she starts to drag it won't be long before we are on the reef ourselves. Tell the engineers to keep the engines on standby."

I went over to the casualty and attended a conference between the master of the ship and the various shore people who turned up – with or without the Indonesians' permission – including the salvage association surveyor. Captain Hancox explained that a bunker barge would be on site in the morning to take off all the bunkers. The ballast and fresh water would be pumped out and ground tackle would be laid.

Early next morning the bunker barge arrived, towed by a Selco tug. It was put alongside the "Frederick Engels" aft where there was water. Ground tackle was laid by Dave Warner and the "Salvista," the Selco mooring and salvage vessel, the ballast and fresh water were pumped out and all was made ready for another attempt on the afternoon's tide. The ability to swing the "Salvaliant" about was limited by the ground tackle and the attempt failed, with no sign of movement.

Salvage, as I was to learn, is an inexact science. By calculation we did not have enough power with the "Salvaliant" and the ground tackle for the ship to refloat. However, on the next afternoon, just as the "Salvaliant" had built up to full power, off she came. The ground tackle was slipped and, when clear of the reef, the "Salvaliant" was slipped. A diving survey was made while the bosun collected our strop and pelican hook.

Shortly afterwards Captain Hancox dismissed us. Peter took the tug to Western Anchorage to clear Immigration and Customs and back to the yard. It had been a fascinating experience, great fun, and we would get a bonus to boot. I was not unhappy with my decision to join Selco.

The refit was finally completed and the first towing job was a barge to Songklha in Thailand. Knobby Halls came with us to make sure all the repairs and improvements worked. I made sure we had a good stock of soda water for him. After delivering the barge we remained in port for a few days. The night life is not as varied as Bangkok!

Back in Singapore Knobby declared himself satisfied with the tug and we went on salvage station in Eastern Anchorage. It was not long before we were ordered to Loyang, where we picked up two crew boats for Brunei. The tow was in fine weather and they were safely delivered.

Communication with Ops was by radio, and a regular schedule was maintained by the radio officer. Ops was manned 24 hours a day. When the radio officer was not on duty there was a speaker turned on in the wheelhouse, with the radio turned on to the calling frequency. The VHF was always switched on to channel 16, the distress frequency. It became second nature to always have one ear listening in, for in the salvage world minutes count. It is often the first tug who reaches a casualty who gets the job.

While anchored off Brunei we received instructions to proceed to a position north and tow a rig. This turned out to be a most demanding job for us, being a single screw tug, and we were in considerable conflict with the tool pusher on the three-legged jack-up rig "Chris Seger". Peter had to try and hold the tug across the current to comply with his instructions while he picked up anchors, and the tool pusher would not agree to any of our suggestions.

Eventually we got under way and with maximum (well, nearly so) power we towed the rig at an average speed of two and a half knots. The rig was finally positioned and anchored and the "Salvaliant" was dismissed. We took the insurance surveyor back to Brunei, plying him with our "Salvaliant" special – which was a particularly lethal gin-based concoction.

We were admiring the sunset when the radio officer handed a message to Peter. He handed me the message on his way to the engine room telephone.

"Two engines maximum power," he ordered into the mouthpiece.

'Drop surveyor. Proceed maximum speed Bombay Reef' read the message. It was signed Bond, a man of few words.

There was a boat waiting at Anchorage to take off the surveyor and Peter turned the tug and headed north along the coast. Bombay Reef was in the South China Sea South of Hong Kong in Chinese territorial waters, but there was a huge area of unsurveyed reefs between us and the reef. It was necessary to steam north to clear the area, and then west out across the China Sea. The weather was fine with a low swell, to which the "Salvaliant" dipped her bow as she thundered along at 15 knots.

Once out in the South China Sea, the North East monsoon was blowing and the tug rolled heavily when the course was altered to the west. Four days after dropping the surveyor we came up on the "Nienberg" in the evening, just as the sun was setting in our eyes, her silhouette black against the red sky. She was aground on the windward side of the reef, with waves breaking around her stern. The remains of a wreck close by – the boiler standing mute and alone – a stark reminder of what would happen to the "Nienberg," some 11,000 gross tons, if we did not get her off.

It was a sombre and serious Peter, all joviality gone, who said, "This is going to be difficult and dangerous, one mistake and we are on the reef ourselves. It's getting dark, there's no way we can make a connection now and it looks too rough to go across in the zed boat. We'll have to wait till morning."

Peter spoke on the VHF radio to the master of the casualty and told him there was nothing we could do until the morning. There was a large communist Chinese vessel to the west, silent and watching. The reef showed up on the radar and Peter steamed the tug round to the south side into the lee, where we spent a comfortable, but for me sleepless, night steaming up and down. I was too tensed up imagining all sorts of horrors for the next day – a line round the propeller or the engines stopped and we drift helplessly onto the reef. This was deep sea ocean salvage and I was glad I was with such an experienced and knowledgeable master.

Peter and I were both on the bridge well before daylight, along with our Filipino officers and bosun. The crew were all out on deck as we steamed back to the "Nienberg", pitching heavily once clear of the lee and then rolling once we headed west. It was getting light now but it was a dismal and sombre dawn with heavy cloud and a grey sea.

Off the casualty Peter dropped back stern first to the reef, pitching into the North East monsoon, while my eyes were glued to the screen of the echo sounder. I shouted out the depths to Peter who was at the monkey island control position. After an hour or so we had a pretty good idea of the depths astern of the "Nienberg". Peter came down to the bridge.

"We'll drop anchor to hold her head into wind and sea, use the rocket gun to fire a line across and pray," he said.

He spoke to the master of the casualty, impressing on him the vital necessity of heaving the tow line across as quickly as possible once they had the messenger. We knew they had power from the lights the ship had displayed the night before.

The anchor was let go near the edge of the reef and Peter manoeuvred stern first towards the casualty where the crew were lining the rails aft. With most of the chain out, the stern of the tug was in shallow water about one cable from the stern of the "Nienberg". We could not get any closer without running aground ourselves. The tug was pitching into the seas, which were still breaking around the stern of the grounded ship. It started to drizzle.

Peter used the engine to ease the weight on the cable. Jesus Armosilla, the second officer, took the Schermuly rocket and line box onto the tow deck, where the tow gear was all ready to be paid out. I was very nervous although, of course, I tried to appear confident in front of the crew. I had never used a rocket gun in my life before. The box and line were neatly laid out on top of the aft hold. I stood on the hatch to gain a little height and steadying myself against the pitch and roll of the tug, I picked up the gun, aimed at the bridge and fired. The bridge and accommodation were aft. There was a loud bang and the line went shooting up in the air towards the casualty. We all watched it with baited breath and a cheer went up as we saw it land near the funnel. Eager hands grabbed it and the messenger coiled on the hatch snaked out over the side, followed by a long polypropylene line.

I glanced up at the rock-like figure standing by the telegraph on the monkey island and Peter gave me a thumbs up sign. The polyprop line floated and it was soon on board the "Nienberg". They put it on the capstan and the line came out of the water as they heaved the towing gear across – wire pendant first, then the stretcher and finally the main tow wire – the joining shackles slipping over the greased towing gunnel. The tow deck was constantly under water as the tug rolled and pitched, but the towline was between the dolly pins – two movable bollards on the towing gunnel – and the propeller was clear.

There was another cheer as the crew on the casualty indicated that they had secured the towing gear. I went forward with the bosun and started to heave up the anchor, Jesus slacked out the main tow wire to Peter's direction. It was vital to keep the tow line reasonably tight so it did not get round the propeller. Once the anchor was aweigh Peter steamed ahead, slacking out the tow wire until about 1,000 feet was out.

"Secure the winch!" he shouted down to Jesus, who acknowledged with a wave of his hand.

"Ring down for two engines," he said to me having returned to the bridge.

Once power was increased the dolly pins were lowered so that the tow wire could run free and swing across the tow deck, enabling the tug to be manoeuvred. The "Salvaliant" was in a most precarious position on the windward side of the reef, now connected to the casualty. If we were unable to stem the current – or anything went wrong – the tug would be on the reef in minutes, the waves breaking over her. It would mean death to many of us. Constant vigilance was required.

Peter spoke to the master of the "Nienberg" on the VHF radio and told him we would have a re-floating attempt. The engines were increased to full power and Peter flung the tug from port to starboard, shipping heavy seas on the tow deck. The casualty used her main engine but reported no movement. After an hour or so the re-floating attempt was stopped and power was reduced on the tug.

'10:30 connected. Refloating attempt made. Failed.' The laconic message Peter sent to the office.

' "Albatross" on the way to assist,' came back a signal from the office.

"All help gratefully received," remarked Peter. "She's pretty heavily aground and we are going to be lucky to get her off."

The Chinese ship was still silent, watching and waiting, her shape indistinct in the drizzle and gloom, as was the boiler on the reef a constant reminder of what could happen.

In the afternoon a vessel was observed coming from the east.

"Wrong way from Singapore if it's the "Albatross"," remarked Peter.

We all watched as the mystery ship came closer and one of our crew said, "It's the "Virginia City"."

"That's the last thing we want here," grumbled Peter.

The "Virginia City" belonged to the Filipino salvage company from Manilla. I looked her up in the Register and saw that she had been built in 1944 – over thirty years ago – was diesel electric and American built.

Jesus spoke to the "Virginia City" in Tagolic on the VHF.

"Cap, they say they have LOF and want to connect," reported Jesus.

"Tell him he can do what he likes but keep clear of us," said Peter.

After the re-floating attempt Peter had manoeuvred the tug up to the west of the "Nienberg" so that the "Salvaliant" was up current. This meant the "Virginia City" would have to connect down current of us thus, if anything went wrong, they would be swept away from the "Salvaliant" rather than on to her.

The "Virginia City" was pitching and rolling in the sea and swell, as was the "Salvaliant", but the tug was pinned down by the tow wire and we were quite comfortable. I felt sorry for the master of the "Virginia City", try as he would he could not make a connection. The tug was bigger than the "Salvaliant" but very slow to manoeuvre and the towing point was much too far aft. Eventually he asked Peter over the radio if he could connect to our bow. I thought Peter was going to explode.

"Hoffre Domma. Does he want to put us on the reef? He will pull us round; our towing gear is not strong enough for two tugs." He was breathing heavily as he opened a can of beer, handing one to me.

"Let me think. Turn that bloody radio off," he growled. He threw the empty beer can into the sea. "OK, Ian, rig the pelican hook on our port bow and make sure that you can get at it to slip in an emergency. We'll make him fast to the pelican hook and once connected I want a man with a hammer standing by 24 hours a day. That is a big, old 'heap of scrap' and I don't want to lose my tug because of him."

"Jesus, tell him to come and connect on our port bow and if he touches us I will shoot him."

Jesus giggled and spoke into the microphone.

The "Virginia City" steamed over towards us. The bosun had his men ready with heaving lines and when the tug steamed slowly past, water pouring off her tow deck as she rolled, they threw them at the tug. One of them was picked up and made fast to the messenger. The "Salvaliant" men quickly heaved it on board, then put it round the windlass drum. The eye of the towing gear was soon on board through the forward fairlead and connected to the pelican hook. The "Virginia City" streamed her gear heading straight out.

"Jesus, tell the "Virginia City" to turn to port and keep up current of us, and then we will have a re-floating attempt."

It failed.

Night fell. It was very dark with a heavily overcast sky. The lights on the "Nienberg" glowed brightly astern, and ahead the dimmer lights of the Filipino tug together with the lights of the Chinese vessel hovering close by. An AB was at the bow with a hammer, standing by the pelican hook.

We steamed all night, monitoring our position on the casualty to make sure we were not swept down current. Peter sent me off to bed at midnight.

Some time later I awoke to a tremendous roar.

"He's pulling us onto the reef, slip slip slip."

I rushed out of my cabin and onto the foredeck. The AB with the hammer gave the pelican hook ring a tremendous hit, it slid off the hook, the hook opened and the "Virginia City" tow wire disappeared out of the fairlead. I looked aft and saw the "Nienberg" up to port.

Jesus, I thought, we are on the reef! I rushed up to the bridge, my heart palpitating in fear, and took a bearing which confirmed my worst thoughts – we had been dragged right down almost onto the reef.

I went into the wheelhouse and found Peter behind the wheel with it hard to port. I could hear the click click of the gyro compass as the heading changed. The "Salvaliant" was clawing her way off the reef. The "Virginia City" steamed off into the night.

"Got rid of the bastard," was all Peter said as he picked up his can of beer.

And that is all I ever found out. Once the tug was back up current and holding her position, Peter said, "All yours, I'm to bed." And he walked off the bridge.

***

I watched the dawn to the east of the "Nienberg", her lights fading in the gathering light, the boiler of the wreck becoming more distinct. I was now used to the motion of the tug, we had been towing for almost 24 hours. The wind was less and the sea seemed to have gone down a little. I studied the stern of the casualty through the big, powerful binoculars on the bridge wing. Only the occasional sea was breaking round the stern but nothing amidships. I watched for some time and began to think it might be possible to get across with a skilful zed boat driver. The "Salvaliant" was equipped with a new, hard-bottomed, rubber zed boat with a 50 horse power outboard.

After an early breakfast I called Peter and told him of what I had observed. He looked his normal self and said, "If you want to have a go, then, OK. But be careful, if you get it wrong you'll be a gonner on the reef."

I called for volunteers and the zed boat was launched. The casualty was warned. Peter told them to put a cargo net over the side and a pilot ladder. I drove the boat with two crew, and stood off the stern to watch.

The entire crew of the "Nienberg" were lining the rails. I

went in at full speed after a wave broke round the stern, rounded up head to sea at the pilot ladder amidships, and with the crew holding onto the cargo net, climbed up the ladder with the painter. As soon as I handed the painter to a "Nienberg" crew member I shouted down for the two crew to follow me. Once they were out of the boat I took the painter forward and moored the boat in the comparatively calm water round the bow.

Elmo, one of the crew who was a diver, had brought a sounding line with him. I told him to take soundings round the ship while I went to see the master.

The "Nienberg" was almost fully laden so had no ballast. She was due to bunker in Singapore so was low on fuel and fresh water. There was no other answer, we would have to jettison the cargo if we were to get her off. I went onto the bridge and talked with Peter on the VHF. He agreed and said he would tell the office. While on the bridge I saw a boat coming from the Chinese ship and they successfully came alongside.

Elmo came up with the sounding plan and with the draughts I had obtained from the master, it confirmed that the ship was very heavily aground and a lot of cargo would have to be jettisoned. I went back to the master's cabin to find three Chinese inside, one of whom was obviously an interpreter and one I guessed was the commissar. They were telling the master that they intended to lay ground tackle. I was aghast. However, as long as it did not interfere with the "Salvaliant", it could do no harm. But how they were going to do it with their great, big ship I did not know.

I went back to the "Salvaliant" in the zed boat. Once having done it, it did not seem so bad and the sea had gone down more. On board I discussed the situation with Peter and studied the cargo plan I brought back. If we could get at the zinc in the lower holds we could lighten her quite quickly.

Peter received a message agreeing to the jettison and at the same time, a weather forecast.

"Hoffre Domma! he exclaimed. "There's a typhoon coming this way, may be four days. That's all we need."

This gave an added urgency to the situation. It was doubtful if the ship would survive a typhoon, and we would have to leave before it arrived if we were to survive ourselves.

I went back to the "Nienberg" with half a dozen crew, together with various kit, and the zed boat driven by a diver returned to bring more. The master agreed to the jettison after I showed him a copy of the message from Selco, and he knew about the typhoon.

Jettison started within the hour and a race against time began. The ship's crew assisted and a boat turned up from the "Tiburon" with more men. I drove a winch and the ship came alive as cargo was lifted out of the holds with the derricks, swung across the deck and thrown over the side. The Chinese commenced work to lay the ground tackle.

Work continued all night, and the next day as well – the "Nienberg" supplying us with food and drink. The zed boat was hoisted on deck, out of the way.

On the fourth afternoon the "Albatross" turned up. We launched the "Salvaliant" zed boat and assisted in making the connection by towing the messenger across. They brought back some tough, burly Germans to help with the jettison.

In the evening the weather started to deteriorate and the sea and swell increased. The typhoon was heading this way and was only a couple of days away.

The next morning the weather had deteriorated so much that it was impossible to use the zed boat, seas were breaking round the stern of the casualty and sweeping along the sides of the ship. We were trapped on board. The typhoon was less than two days away.

I discussed with Peter over the radio what we should do, apart from continue the jettison as quickly as possible.

"It is possible she may come off as the swell moves in from the typhoon. We are probably feeling it now," he said, "if she won't come off by the time I have to leave, you will have to ballast her down, batten down the hatches and pray. You are trapped on board."

"All understood," I said. "We've jettisoned almost one thousand tons now and when standing on the stern, there are definite signs of movement as the seas hit the stern."

"That's a good sign. We will have a last attempt at 16:00." He signed off.

I spoke with the Germans from the "Albatross" and the Filipinos from the "Virginia City" and told them the plan. I spoke with the master and asked him how the Chinese intended to slip their ground tackle wire. There did not appear to be a plan, so I asked him to have cutting gear standing by nearby.

At 16:00 I left the jettisoning and went to the bridge. The "Salvaliant" was towing to the west and the "Albatross" down current to the east. The Chinese ground tackle wire was still further down current. The two tugs increased to full power, I could see the boiling water round their sterns from the propellers. The tow wires were bar taut. In unison the two tugs started sheering to port and then to starboard, heeling as they moved sideways through the sea, water cascading off their tow decks. The "Nienberg" engine was put full astern. On the third swing to port there was definite movement, the "Nienberg" swung a few degrees and stopped. The ground tackle was holding her.

"Ian." I heard my name over the radio. "Cut the ground tackle wire."

The "Salvaliant" welder was amongst the jettison party but I told him to standby at the ground tackle when I left the hold. I ran down to the after deck and told him to cut the wire. He lit the cutting gear and put it on the wire. It was bar taut, humming with the strain. I stood behind him to lend moral support. If you stand at the point of parting, the broken wire will not hit you. It took courage to cut that wire. Some Chinese was gabbling away but I took no notice.

Suddenly there was the sound of a gun going off. The wire parted and one end disappeared over the side, taking part of the rail with it, the other shorter end flung itself backwards inboard hitting a winch. The welder and I were clear standing at the point of breakage. The "Nienberg" started swinging rapidly to port, the stern towards the towing tugs, and then there was a tremendous bang and we were almost thrown off our feet. She was moving. She stopped and again there was a bang, and then she started pounding and moving astern.

I raced back onto the bridge. The shuddering and pounding stopped, she was afloat.

"Stop the engine," I ordered, and the telegraph was put to stop.

The "Nienberg" was rolling in the swell as she swung broadside onto the swell. The jettisoning stopped and the crews were cheering.

"Ian, let go of the "Albatross" first and then me," instructed Peter over the radio, "and then steam round to the south side of the reef."

The "Salvaliant" crew were already at the towing connections when I went back aft. We let go the two tugs without difficulty and I went back onto the bridge.

"I will pilot you round to the other side of the reef," I told the master.

"Slow ahead," I ordered. "Hard a port," I instructed the man at the wheel, and walked to the radar. It was almost dark but as on the "Salvaliant", the reef showed up on the radar.

The two tugs were recovering their towing gear, their bright deck lights illuminating their tow decks. The "Nienberg" was rolling heavily in the sea and swell; the hatches were open, loose gear rolled around on deck, but it was not long before I altered south and then west into the lee of the reef.

There were mutual congratulations all round, even the Chinese smiled. The ship's crew and salvage crew closed the hatches and lowered the derricks. We were all keen to steam south as quickly as possible, out of the path of the typhoon.

The carpenter reported there was no leakage in the holds or tanks. The ship was sound. The chief engineer reported the engines to be in good order.

It was about 21:00 when I finally reached the "Salvaliant" with the termination letter. I sat on the bridge with a beer and was suddenly engulfed by tiredness. I'd had no sleep for more than two days and much of that time I had been jettisoning cargo.

We watched the "Nienberg" get under way and followed her

on two engines to keep up and get south as quickly as possible.

The next morning the "Nienberg" was out of sight to the south and we were well clear of the typhoon. Peter slowed down to economical speed.

A couple of days later we received a message to proceed to a position off the East Malaysian Coast amongst the reefs in the unsurveyed area. The weather was fine and we proceeded at full speed.

We arrived during the morning to find the salvage vessel "Salviper" alongside and the salvage crew discharging rubber bales onto a barge. Captain Hancox was in charge but after helping to discharge for a day, we received instructions to proceed to Singapore.

***

In Singapore we went on salvage standby in Eastern Anchorage. This was the boring part of salvage – waiting for something to happen. You don't know when it will occur. If I went ashore I had a pager if available and if not, I had to phone Ops and tell them where I was. So if I went to two bars and a restaurant, each time I moved I had to phone in. If there was an emergency they would phone and I would get back to the tug as quickly as possible, usually within the hour. There were always plenty of bumboats at Clifford Pier. It was the same for the crew and only a limited number were allowed ashore at any one time.

On board, the Selco channel and VHF channel 16 were monitored all the time. Peter stayed at home most nights but he could be picked up with the zed boat within twenty minutes.

Eastern Anchorage was interesting from a shipping point of view because of the variety of shipping anchored there.

I met Mr Kahlenberg a few times in the office and he was especially pleased about the "Nienberg", which was a very good salvage. He was always very friendly, albeit always very busy.

On Christmas Eve I received a message over the Selco network to proceed to Mr Kahlenberg's house. When I reached the shore I had to phone Ops to find out where it was so I could tell the driver. Even so it was difficult to find in the dark.

I walked up the drive once the watchman let me in and was sweating when I arrived at the door. A maid let me in to the air-conditioned house and I found Mr K, as he was more affectionately known, or EEK which were his initials, sitting in a large armchair in the wooden-floored drawing-room. There were lots of Christmas decorations, with a large Christmas tree in the corner.

"Good evening, Captain Tew," greeted Mr K.

Promotion at last, I thought.

"Sit down and have a drink. We celebrate Christmas Eve rather than Christmas Day."

The maid brought me a beer. I was on my best behaviour; there were no other guests and not everyone gets to have a drink with the chairman in his house.

A short, stout middle-aged lady came into the room and Mr K introduced his wife, Hilda, as I stood up and shook hands. She sat down and was silent as Mr K and I chatted about salvage.

About ten minutes later a lively, well-dressed young lady entered the room and I was introduced to Marie Louise, the Kahlenberg's daughter.

Shortly afterwards we all went into dinner at a beautifully set table with flowers and candles. It was the traditional roast goose with lots of wine. It turned out to be a very jolly evening, all the more so because it was so unexpected; one minute sitting on the tug, the next in the chairman's Christmas-decorated house eating roast goose with his family!

There was no salvage, so I spent Christmas Day at Alan Bond's open house, and got to know a lot more Selco personnel: Chris Herbert – festooned as usual with radios and gadgets – a very large man indeed, accompanied by his partner; Knobby Halls and Anne; Dave Warner and his wife and children; David Hancox and his Japanese wife, Akiko; Peter and Unke with Peter and Caroline; Daniel Boon, the personnel man, someone to keep in with if I wanted a particular crew; Ismael Bin Dollah, in charge of Ops, a most important man. Mr K turned up on his own. There were various other non-Selco people, in particular the salvage association chief surveyor and other shoreside people involved in tugs and barges and salvage.

I spent the next six months with Peter but there was not another "Nienberg", although we still performed a few salvage jobs and a few false alarms. There was nothing worse than having an emergency only to find the competition arrived first, or the ship was no longer in distress.

We towed a Greek cargo ship in ballast from the middle of the Malacca Straits, but it was a contract job so no bonus. We assisted in putting out a fire on a ship in Eastern Anchorage, but the Port fire tug was there as well – and our competitors – and the fire was out very quickly, so not much excitement.

One night there was a collision in the Singapore Straits off Eastern Anchorage. I had the anchor aweigh as Peter climbed on board from the zed boat and he took her at full speed in the dark through the Anchorage and out into the Straits.

He went straight alongside the burning loaded tanker and we started fighting the fire which was raging forward, the flames leaping out from the forecastle. The "Salvaliant" was made fast on the starboard shoulder. Two salvage crew worked the fire monitors above the monkey island, playing jets of water over the forecastle. I was on the deck of the tanker, with the rest of our crew playing fire hoses from the tug at the furiously burning fire. I was very conscious we were standing on top of loaded tanks, the occasional smell of crude oil giving added urgency to our fire fighting efforts.

At one stage there was a tremendous bang, the crew all ran aft and I fell on the deck thinking there had been an explosion. The door to the paint room had blown open and flames leapt out. Once I had collected my wits together I stood up, signalled to my crew to pick up the hoses, and advance on the flames. We soon put it out and after four hours, the fire in the forecastle was extinguished.

The messman kept us well supplied with cold drinks – Peter slipping in a couple of cold beers for me – for it was a hot, tropical night apart from the heat of the fire. Just as we put the fire out the "Salviper" turned up, the ship she was attending sank. We were not very pleased with Captain Hancox muscling in on our salvage after the fire was out and sharing in the salvage bonus.

Dave Hancox, the dour Australian, was a Walter Mitty type character. He imagined he had done things, and really believed it, when, in fact, they were figments of his fertile imagination. It was very difficult to tell fact from fiction. For instance, he said that the fire on the sunk ship had been so intense it had melted his wheelhouse windows, but the "Salviper" windows were intact. He said the "Salviper" had been surrounded by burning oil but there were no scorch marks on the pristine paint or burnt rubber on the rubber fenders. He continually told stories of how he fought in the Vietnam War; well, he had been there but on a salvage job not fighting. However, once you filtered out the fiction, Dave was a very knowledgeable salvor and in general helped me a lot.

A large tanker ran aground in the sand banks off one Fathom Bank at the entrance to the Malacca Straits. This was a major salvage on Lloyd's Open Form and half the Selco fleet turned up. Part of the crude oil cargo was to be discharged before she could be refloated.

Captain Hancox was in charge of the salvage and he was in command of the salvage vessel "Salviper". We stood by with the "Salvaliant" connected to the casualty ready to tow after the ground tackle was laid laid. A small tug and barge arrived, loaded with equipment and fenders needed for the lightening operation. The crew boat "Salvital" arrived with an assortment of surveyors and owners' representatives.

I used another tug and our zed boat, with a portable echo sounder to find a way out through the banks once the tanker was refloated. I felt like an explorer of old and was pleased with the result. I piloted the lightening tanker and put her alongside the grounded ship, which was should we say stimulating not having manoeuvred anything larger than a salvage tug. It was a satisfactory first for me and I was grateful to Captain Hancox for giving me the responsibility.

After a few days the tanker was successfully refloated and

the lightened cargo reloaded. I piloted the salved vessel through the channel I had found, back into the Straits and south to Singapore.

A fully laden Indian tanker, the "Lal Bahadur Shastri", ran aground on Helen Mar Reef on the Indonesian side of the Singapore Straits. This was another LOF salvage with ground tackle being laid by the "Salvista". Captain Hancox was in charge, the "Salviper" providing support. The "Salvital" brought out *The Straits Times* each day.

The "Salvaliant" was connected and numerous small tugs turned up with personnel and equipment. I piloted the lightening ship alongside and took her off again when loaded – not easy in the strong cross current but assisted by Selco tugs.

During these salvage operations I kept good notes, so was able to give evidence to Dennis Rixon when he came out. This was sometimes an ordeal if he was in a bad mood and he never stopped reminding me I was given the job on his recommendation. Mr K depended on him to a great extent in the legal work, so I had to put up with Dennis. On the other hand he could be charming and we had some very pleasant dinners together, and Sunday lunches with EEK.

Dennis was a baby-faced, thick, stocky man with an endless fund of jokes which he regaled the assembled company, or it might be only me, over numerous beers. When diabetes was diagnosed he was even more difficult and irritable, especially when he was on the wagon for a day or two. However, it greatly assisted my career for my evidence to turn up at arbitrations in London and my name became known amongst the arbitrators and QCs involved in the salvage world.

The "Showa Maru" was one of the biggest Lloyd's Open Form salvage operations of its day. This Japanese tanker ran aground in the Singapore Straits on the Indonesian side on the way to Japan loaded with 250,000 tons of crude oil, breaching her tanks and polluting the Straits. People turned up from London and Tokyo to advise on the pollution, but the best thing in these circumstances to limit pollution is to salve the ship, which today's environmentalists seem to forget.

Captain Hancox was in charge and I became his assistant,

living on the "Showa Maru" for five weeks. Once ground tackle was laid from all four corners of the ship the "Salvaliant" was dismissed. I remained, being Captain Hancox's assistant, living with one of the new Motorolas Chris Herbert bought which worked inside the ship. I could communicate with Ops, or any of the tugs, or Dave Hancox 24 hours a day wherever I was located.

The ship was opened up along her bottom and some of the crude oil was lost, but as soon as a water bottom was established the leakage stopped. It was necessary to lighten her to refloat.

A small Shell tanker was chartered to lighten the "Showa Maru" while she was aground and shuttle the crude oil to a larger tanker for transport on to Japan. Yokohama fenders, huge floating rubber fenders, were used for the tankers to lie alongside both the "Showa Maru" and the larger tanker anchored off. Selco tugs were used to assist in the berthing operations.

The piping system on the casualty was damaged during the grounding so special hydraulically-driven submersible pumps were flown in from the States, along with their Coast Guard operating crews. These were used to pump the crude oil out of the tanks 'over the top' and into the ship's manifold, where it was discharged into the lightening tanker. Selco Salvage crews assisted the United States Coast Guard teams, kept watch on the ground tackle, the mooring lines between the ships, the fenders and the many other multitudinous jobs that were required to be done.

Captain Hancox and his advisers – consultants from London – calculated the discharge sequence so that the damaged hull did not break up. I spent a lot of time with him, learnt a lot, and supervised the salvage crews.

She was successfully refloated with the "Salvaliant" and assisting tugs, and anchored. A full discharge was required so that the ship could be dry docked, and this was done at anchor. Finally, the "Salvaliant", looking very small from the bridge of the now empty "Showa Maru", towed her to off the dry dock where she was anchored and the termination letter was signed.

It was late at night when I came ashore in the "Salvital" with the Japanese owners' representative and Captain Hancox. We were met in the otherwise deserted office by Mr K who gave us an enthusiastic welcome and congratulations. Dave, as dour as ever, refused EEK's invitation to his house and went off. The Japanese representative and I accompanied Mr K to his house, where neither Hilda nor Marie Louise were very pleased to see us at 1:00 in the morning!

Nothing loath, Ernie set to and we had scrambled eggs and tinned oysters, washed down with champagne as a celebratory supper. After all, Selco had achieved a world coup in the salvage world and the Japanese were glad to have their ship back safely salved. It is true to say that Selco made a lot of money and I received a large salvage bonus so, all in all, everyone was happy.

SALVIKING MY FIRST COMMAND

I was promoted master of the new Selco-built salvage and mooring vessel "Salviking". Captain at last at the age of 32! There is no other feeling in the world than being master of your own ship, or at least that is the way I felt. It was *my* ship and *my* crew and I was very proud of my first command. I had a crew of almost thirty, it varied a bit depending on what job we were performing.

Tony Church was acting master on sea trials which were not yet completed, so the first time I took her out was on trials. I needed a tug to tow her out of the base but soon got used to handling this flat-bottomed ship, with her horns for mooring work sticking out ahead. The bridge was aft and the working deck stretched ahead, with the huge salvage mooring winch beneath the wheelhouse and the 30 ton derrick just forward. Her length was 200 feet and beam 20 feet and her comparatively shallow draught was 10 feet. The trials were successfully completed and I went out with Tony for a few beers.

I knew nothing about mooring work and the first job with the "Salviking" was to overhaul the Port Dickson mooring and buoys. Luckily Charles Deeney had joined Selco and he was an expert, so he came along in charge of the mooring work.

The short voyage round to Port Dickson in the Malacca Straits was made without incident, the divers coming by land. The chains were lifted, inspected and relaid. I found the work incredibly boring and left it to Charles, manoeuvring the "Salviking" whenever required.

Once the mooring job was completed, I received a message to proceed north up the Malacca Straits 'on spec'. Unfortunately, the 'spec' did not require assistance, so I headed south back to Singapore. On the way the weather blew up, as it can in the Malacca Straits, to about force 7. With the blunt bows the sea came on deck which, under normal circumstances, would not have mattered – running off through the scuppers. Unfortunately, water got below in the hold which reduced the freeboard, causing more water to come on board. I turned and ran before the wind with the sea astern until it moderated, then continued back to Singapore.

It turned out that the rubber packing, which should have made the hatch watertight, was missing. The hatch was situated in the middle of, and was flush with, the working deck so any water coming over the bow went straight down the side of the hatch. I received a letter from Mr Bond blaming me for this and was incensed – the vessel having just been surveyed by NKK, the Japanese classification society – and passed by Captain Hancox, who was acting superintendent in charge of the "Salviking".

When I went to remonstrate with Bond he simply said, "You are the master, it's your responsibility to check the vessel is seaworthy. Don't try and blame other people."

The first salvage operation I performed with the "Salviking" was at Batam in Indonesia, just across the Straits from Singapore. Dave Warner, with his red hair and permanently sunburnt face, with four divers accompanied us. I moored the ship with the horns forward over the sunken tug and the divers put wire strops round her, being careful to parcel the wires at the edges so the sunken craft was not 'cheesed'. She weighed about seventy tons and the "Salviking" 's bow was almost under water when the salvage mooring winch was put in double gear and the lift commenced. When the tug was at the surface, portable electric pumps were put on board and the water pumped out. As the level fell in the engine room so the machinery was preserved from the effects of salt water.

Fernando Legaspi, middle-aged and small, was my chief engineer and he knew the "Salviking" engines inside out because he rebuilt them. Arturo Briosi was my chief officer, a well trained salvage man from the "Salviper", stocky and strong. Pepe, tall and knowledgeable, also ex "Salviper", was the bosun. John, an Indian, dark and intelligent, was my radio officer. The welder, nicknamed Ikan, was a whiz kid at fixing things. There were three permanent divers with their kit; four fitters in the engine room; six able seamen on deck; two deck officers; and two engineers. All in all, a well manned salvage vessel.

After our tug-raising job, I proceeded back to Singapore to prepare for a pipe pulling job in Indonesia. I was not that keen because this sort of work did not really interest me but Peter was in command of the "Salvaliant" and Selco, at that time, did not have any more big tugs. So I held my peace.

The amount of equipment for this pipe pull was immense and included over a mile of wire with which to pull the pipe; the sledge on which the edge of the pipe would be made fast; drums to assist the pipe to float; bottles of oxy acetyline; boxes of welding rods; beer; soft drinks and tinned food for six months; and a full freezer. When all was on board, including the 15 ton "Charlie Brown" work boat, the "Salviking" was overloaded, but I turned a blind eye despite Bond's letter!

I departed early in the New Year 1975 bound for Balik Papan. The quickest route was out past Horsburgh Lighthouse at the entrance to the Singapore Straits and across open sea to the Southern end of Indonesian Borneo. I wished I had gone the sheltered route via the Bangka Straits.

Half a day past Horsburgh Light it blew up fresh and in the night, blew a full gale. The heavily laden "Salviking" laboured, shipping heavy seas across the deck and rolled. I slowed down to the minimum speed possible to keep steerage way and hove to but she still seemed to be almost permanently under water and even when I put her bow to sea, she rolled.

It was a dark overcast night with no stars visible, just white horses bearing down on the ship. I was distinctly apprehensive with the behaviour of the salvage vessel and it did not help when some drums broke loose and were eventually lost overboard. There was too much water on the foredeck for anybody to go out. I had been at sea in much worse weather: "Anatina" off Iceland; "Eastern Maid" in the China Sea; "Eastern Ranger" off Korea; but I had never before been apprehensive about the ship. I frankly thought we might be overwhelmed but, of course, did not voice my fears to anyone and kept up a cheerful demeanour all night, sustained by cups of coffee.

It did not look a lot better in daylight and I remained hove to. About noon the weather moderated, and by evening the "Salviking" was back on economical speed.

Indonesia was corrupt, and if one is to operate there you have to accept that fact and bribe. If you don't nothing happens and you cannot start, let alone complete, a contract. Naturally this was allowed for when bidding.

In Balik Papan, which was a one-eyed place, the "Salviking" was held up for the 'cargo' to be checked. The person who was supposed to have 'arranged' all this did not turn up so the right palm was not been greased. Eventually we were cleared in and the permit to stay and work in Indonesia issued. Our contract was with Pertamina so you would have thought there would be no problems but, as I said, Indonesia was corrupt. However, having got 'in' to Indonesia the next problem was to be allowed to leave Balik Papan and eventually, after a few more wasted days, I was given the 'clearance'. If nothing else, the weather was fine but hot and even the night club seemed quite fun.

I steamed up the coast north-bound in fine weather, the occasional country craft being the only traffic, the coast covered in thick, green jungle. It was hot and sticky outside, but the bridge was air-conditioned so I did not improve my sun tan.

There was nothing at Sangatta, literally nothing – it was coordinates on the chart. Mr Panigada, Paddy for short, was setting up a base camp to live, and trestles on which to weld the pipes. I anchored the "Salviking" offshore where there was no shelter.

We were there for six months. There were delays and more delays but eventually the pipe was pulled, with the "Salviking" moored a mile offshore. The pipe was in sections. As each section was welded, the welds tested and inspected, we would pull that section and then wait for the next section to be welded on. The trick was not to allow the pipe to sink into the mud, otherwise it took a lot of pulling to unstick it, especially when almost a mile was on the bottom. We finished up with the pipe one foot out from its planned position.

Charles Deeney turned up to do the mooring and seven months after leaving Balik Papan, we returned. It seemed like a great bustling, glistening metropolis after more than half a year at Sangatta.

Our troubles were only just beginning because the Indonesians would not let us go. Obviously the right palms were not greased and time seemed to be of no object. The ostensible reason for not giving us a clearance was that we were not leaving with the same 'cargo' we had arrived with. Well, that was not surprising because we had eaten the food and most of the deck cargo formed the pipe and mooring system at Sangatta!

John, the radio officer, handed me a message one Friday morning.

'Obtain clearance and proceed maximum speed to coordinates north of Balik Papan.' Signed Bond.

Easier said than done in Indonesia which is a Moslem country. I found the agent, loaded the car with cold beer and made the rounds of all the officials to obtain a clearance to sail for a vessel in distress. The officials were not very interested in the distress, only how much we were prepared to pay! We obtained the clearance by the end of the day only by guaranteeing to return and considerable bribes. "Charlie Brown" was left behind and I sailed in the evening just as it was getting dark. It had been a long day and there was not much beer left in the car!

I returned in five days. Our Filipino competitors were given the job.

The next couple of weeks were spent salving some barges with Charlie Brown, which was quite fun.

***

One evening, before going ashore to the night club, John said there was a telephone call for me on the radio from UK. I was most surprised. My father had died. It was a bolt totally out of the blue and I was sad and sorry I had not seen him for two years. We had got on well enough and he had always been there for me.

I sent a message to Singapore asking for a relief so I could attend the funeral. I flew from Balik Papan to Djakarta and thence to Singapore, handing over the "Salviking" in the bar of the Orchid Inn. I caught the 22:00 flight to Heathrow, where I hired a car and drove home. It is strange the efforts made to honour the dead, yet cannot make the effort to visit the living.

The funeral was at Stoke Fleming, taken by his Godson, John Giles, son of Jack Giles. Dad's father was vicar at St Peters between 1913 to 1915 when he died from a riding accident. Dad was buried in the family grave with his parents, which has a magnificent view overlooking Start Bay. The sunlight glinted on the sea from which he had drawn his living, being a naval architect, and his pleasure – small boat sailing. The post funeral party was held at Gunfield Boathouse in Dartmouth, with its panoramic view up harbour towards the Naval College, which dominates the harbour.

At this time, Donald was a manager with Bristol and West Building Society, the job with Herbert having folded with the collapse of the stock market – "Anatina" and the estate in Scotland being sold. Edward was a major with the Royal Engineers, Malcolm was a flight lieutenant, and James was a lieutenant in the Navy.

SALVALIANT IN COMMAND

I flew back to Singapore and took command of the "Salvaliant", Peter having taken command of the new big Selco tug "Salvanquish". The tug was full of old faces amongst the crew: bosun – tough, dependable Javier Patani; cook – scruffy, dark Conrad Diotay; divers – tough, big Paquito Delos Rey and good-looking Elmo Ramos; welder – Ikan from the Salviking. Jesus Armosilla was still the chief officer and Edgar Selorio was the second. Middle-aged Fernando was still the chief engineer, and most of the engine room crew were the same. The tug had almost become a family.

The "Salvaliant" was equipped with only a single drum tow winch, which meant it was difficult to tow more than one ship at once. The tug was contracted to tow the Royal Fleet Auxiliary tanker "Green Ranger" to Hong Kong and the ex Strick Line ship "Foochow" to Canton, both going for scrap.

The North East monsoon was blowing strongly according to the weather forecasts I received. We rigged the tows in Western Anchorage. The "Salvaliant" was alongside the "Foochow" in the 69 position and when the salvage association surveyor was satisfied with the preparations, Dave Hancox turned up on the "Salviper" with an old boiler as reservoir and a large compressor. There was no power on the tow so the anchor was heaved up using air instead of steam. I towed the "Foochow" out of Anchorage and streamed the tow, keeping it short for the passage through Singapore main strait.

Meanwhile, Dave sailed off with the boiler and compressor to lift the anchor of the "Green Ranger", which was being towed with the "Salvanquish," Peter in command. Off Eastern Anchorage Peter caught up and brought the "Salvanquish" alongside the "Salvaliant" – our rubber tyre fenders sufficient in the smooth waters of the Strait. The "Foochow" was on the main tow wire which was slacked out allowing room for the

"Green Ranger," which was on the fixed wire. The fixed wire was passed over to the "Salvaliant" and made fast. I now had two tows and increased to full speed. Once Peter saw that all was well he wished me luck over the radio, blew three blasts on the whistle and proceeded back to Singapore. Both the tows followed very well and by midnight we were passing Horsburgh Light and out into the South China Sea.

Although it was longer, the Palawan Passage route – recommended by the salvage association – called for proceeding up the coast of Borneo, East Malaysia and the Philippines, then crossing the South China Sea with the weather on the beam to Hong Kong. I say 'recommended', which is the official word, but if I did not follow this route the tow would be uninsured, so it is more like an instruction. However, this is the Admiralty recommended route for low powered vessels and I agreed with it.

The tow proceeded well until I started crossing the South China Sea with the weather just forward of the beam. Once clear of the lee of the Philippines, the sea and swell got up and the wind increased until it was blowing a gale. The tug rolled heavily and was most uncomfortable. The towing gunnel was regularly greased to protect the tow wires. Progress was slow but the "Salvaliant "carried over 600 tons of fuel so that was no problem.

On a dark night south of Scarborough Reef the engine revs suddenly increased a little more than the usual change with the pitch and roll of the tug. I walked out onto the bridge wing and looked aft. I only had one tow, the "Green Ranger" had gone. My heart sank. I walked back onto the bridge and looked at the radar screen; there she was, the distance slowly increasing.

The bosun came onto the bridge dripping wet. "Wire broken, Cap," he said, "all gone." So at least nothing was hanging over the side.

'Green Ranger broken adrift. North-east gale. Coordinates....' Signed Tew.

That was the message I sent when I called the radio officer. I sat down to think what to do. I could just abandon the tow, which was the easy thing to do, and send out a navigational warning. Even having lost a tow, the "Salvaliant" was not making a lot of progress and it was rough.

I told Jesus to ring down and tell the engine room to reduce slowly to half speed. I watched the "Foochow" through the binoculars, her outline just visible in the dark and the red sidelight.

The "Salvaliant" was almost stopped in the water and we were lying quite comfortably, but the "Green Ranger" was drifting away quite rapidly.

I finally made up my mind. I would stand by the "Green Ranger" and wait for the weather to moderate, then try and pick her up and reconnect the tow. I would not send a navigational warning, which would bring out rival salvage tugs who would try and pick her up and take her off me. I told the chief officer to warn the bosun I was going to turn and steam downwind, following the "Green Ranger" until we could pick her up again.

"OK, Cap," he acknowledged.

The turn went all right, although the tug rolled horribly, and with the tug going slowly, the "Foochow" followed – drifting beam onto the wind.

We waited four days, slowly drifting back towards Singapore. The weather finally moderated enough to make an attempt possible to pick up the tow. A fishing boat appeared and went towards the "Green Ranger" about half a mile away. I blew the whistle and increased speed. They continued and went alongside the drifting ship. I was beside myself with rage, this was my ship and no one was going to take her away from me.

I continued to blow the whistle, my crew were all on deck now shouting and waving at the fishing boat. They took no notice and one crew started to climb on board using the emergency towing wire. I rushed down into my cabin, snatched the rifle out of my wardrobe. I opened the safe and grabbed the revolver and all the ammunition and returned to the bridge. We were close now and one man was on board with another following him up the wire.

"Anyone know how to use these things?" I asked.

Ricky, the radio officer, took the rifle and loaded it while Jesus did the same with the revolver.

"Point it at them and shoot," I ordered Ricky.

Suddenly there was a *rat-a-tat* like a machine gun going off and bullets sprayed onto the "Green Ranger". I took the revolver off Jesus and fired a couple of shots but it was unnecessary. The two men on the "Green Ranger" shot back into their boat, which took off at high speed back towards Manila. Ricky had the rifle on automatic instead of single shot, but it had had the desired effect. The crew were all whooping and laughing with glee.

The next problem to solve was how to pick up the "Green Ranger" while still towing the "Foochow". I could not go astern on the engine or I would have the tow line round the propeller, and I could not stop for too long or the tug might drift over the "Foochow" tow line. I eventually came to the conclusion that the only way to do it was to put the ships on different tacks. The "Green Ranger" was heading about southeast so if I turned the "Foochow" so she was heading northwest there would be time to pick up the drifting ship before the "Foochow" turned on her tow wire and came drifting back to collide with us. This is what I did and the crew were fantastic at picking up the emergency tow wire and bridle rigged along the side of the "Green Ranger" and connecting it to a new fixed tow wire.

" "Green Ranger" reconnected." I gave Ricky the message to send to Singapore as the tug and tows picked up speed.

I sat down to enjoy a beer, well pleased with myself and the crew.

I later wrote an article for the Nautical Institute Magazine describing the pick up and claimed it as a world first and no one to date has disputed it.

Off Hong Kong I delivered the "Green Ranger" to the scrapyard tugs and continued onto the entrance of the Pearl River. A pilot boarded, along with a commissar, and it was quite obvious that the pilot knew nothing about towing. A tug was made fast on either side of the "Foochow" and, instead of the nice placid tow she had been – following meekly behind the tug – she became a wild thing sheering from side to side.

The pilot was gabbling instructions into the radio and I realised we were not going to get up the river like this. It was quite wide at the entrance but it became progressively narrower the further up one proceeded. I decided to take charge. I instructed the pilot to tell the two tugs to stop their engines. Immediately the "Foochow" started to behave herself. The pilot seemed most surprised.

Once things were settled I took the pilot and commissar down to the spare cabin, which contained a fridge full of beer, and suggested they might like to relax and I would call them when I wanted help.

I had the Admiralty chart of the river and followed the buoys up to Canton, the tow behaving perfectly following the tug. I called the pilot just before reaching the city and asked him where we were supposed to drop off the tow. He looked as though he had had a good time with the contents of the fridge! The tide was making and he said we had to anchor, so I turned the "Foochow" head to tide, sent the zed boat across with a salvage crew and they let go the anchor. Lots of people turned up but I got my delivery letter signed and disconnected the tow. I went alongside the tow to collect all our equipment and spend the night.

The next morning our clearance and a pilot turned up and I proceeded down the river, the pilot navigating! I dropped him off at the entrance of the Pearl River and steamed in the back way to Hong Kong, past the outlying islands. I took up salvage station in the harbour, with the view of Hong Kong Island and the Peak visible on fine days. The "Foochow" was the largest ship at that time ever to have been towed dead up the Pearl river, a mini world first.

The green painted Star Ferries, plying to Kowloon side, and the black Yaumati car ferries, running to the islands, created a continuous wash – augmented by the occasional ship passing by. White painted jet foils run on Boeing aero engines, hydro foils and conventional ferries, ran to Macau. The harbour was a little smaller from my Indo China days for there had been a lot of infilling on the Hong Kong side, so the tide ran a little stronger.

Our agents were Everett Steamship Corporation and the head men were English. I became particularly friendly with John Davison, who had been in British India Steamship Navigation Co Ltd. I first met him in Calcutta when I was cadet and he was a second officer. He was married to a Chinese lady and had a son. We enjoyed many a convivial lunch or dinner.

Marie Louise, Ernie's daughter, was the Selco representative in Hong Kong and she worked in an office in Everetts. We also had a few convivial lunches and dinners together, sometimes alone and sometimes with people connected to the salvage world.

Hong Kong was a thriving, bustling, busy place. Everyone wore suits to work and you could not get into the best places unless you were properly dressed, so I had a couple of suits made.

Salvage station is incredibly boring but I had a pager and arranged a couple for the crew so we could get ashore. I also had an international telephone put on the bridge so we could be in instant communication with Singapore. My time was much enlivened by Marie Louise and the Everett people.

The worst bully on the "Chindwara" was a man called Thorn and in discussion with John it turned out that he was in Hong Kong as a surveyor. He had lost a ship on Pratas Reef, between Taiwan and Hong Kong, in bad weather and was now ashore. John knew all about the "Chindwara" and thought it would be a good idea if we met and laid the ghosts of the past to rest. I was not so sure but John assured me he was not a bad guy, which was not my recollection.

John arranged a lunch-time meeting in the cellar bar under the Connaught Centre, which was the office watering hole. Lunch extended to an evening drink and dinner and the ghosts were, indeed, laid to rest – along with an appalling hangover the next day. He was not so bad after all and told me how they had all been hauled over the coals on the "Chindwara" and the bullying was stopped.

Marie Louise obtained a contract for us to tow a passenger

ship which was lying at the scrapyard to Manila. I took the tug over to Junk Bay and made my initial inspection. She was an ex Silver Line ship – my old school friend, Johnathen Priest, was with them – and it was eerie walking through the empty, silent, deserted ship. I felt if I had a magic wand I could suddenly make her come alive; everything was in place, all it needed was people and power.

The tug was anchored in the bay and I returned to bring her alongside the reprieved ship. While approaching I was standing at the manoeuvring position on the monkey island and put the telegraph from half ahead to slow astern. Not only did nothing happen, the engine revs increased. I put the telegraph to full astern. I was heading straight for the white hull of the passenger ship. The engine, instead of stopping and going astern, increased revs to full ahead. I was now steaming at full ahead with the telegraph at full astern and, realising something was wrong, put the helm hard over to starboard. I gave the emergency double ring astern on the telegraph but got even more revs ahead.

I shouted at Jesus to phone down to the engine room and get the engine astern quick before we collided with our tow-to-be. The "Salvaliant" slowly started to turn, and with my heart in my mouth, she scraped past the ship at full speed with inches to spare and back out into the bay. I put the telegraph to stop and the engine stopped.

Shaking with fear and gibbering with rage, I let the tug drift while I ranted and raved at the chief engineer. Poor Fernando had never seen me so angry before and I hope never to lose my temper like that again. Eventually I calmed down enough to apologise, for although Fernando made the initial mistake I compounded it. As soon as I realised there was a wrong way engine movement I should have put the telegraph to stop. The messman brought me a cold beer and we tried again and went alongside with no problem.

It was a rough trip down to Manila but the tow went very well. We did not spend long before returning to Hong Kong for Christmas and more partying. My step-cousin, David Wynne Davis, was stationed in Hong Kong with the army and

I took him out to dinner in the Eagle's Nest at the Hilton Hotel, with its view over Hong Kong. He invited me to a Beating Retreat, which was nostalgic and poignant with the sun setting over China. I also took him for dinner at the top of the Hilton, which was good but expensive – not surprising from a hotel classed as one of the best in the world.

I was intending to go to Midnight Mass at the cathedral but my pager went off and I missed out, and it was not even a salvage!

The "Salvaliant" acted as an 'anchor' for a barge while the towing tug went into dry dock in January 1976. It was cold and I was glad when that boring job was over and I received instructions over the phone from Singapore to proceed to Brunei at economical speed. For a long time I wanted to land on Scarborough Reef, which was on the way, having passed it many times on the 'H' boats.

I proceeded at full speed from Hong Kong and stopped off at the reef, the divers surveying a suitable spot to anchor in the lee.

We spent a most enjoyable six hours in bright sunshine snorkelling and swimming on the reef. I sat on the bridge in the setting sun eating fresh crayfish caught by the divers, washed down with a good white wine.

I continued at economical speed, arriving at the "Runna" at the time given in my original ETA from Hong Kong, no one any the wiser of our little rest and recreation!

The "Runna" was a loaded log carrier with an engine problem. She was to be towed dead ship without any crew on board, and my salvage crew prepared her for towing and rigged the towing gear. We lifted the anchor ourselves and got under way without any assistance. The voyage up the Palawan Passage went very well in fine weather; the "Runna", being loaded, yawed about a bit but nothing to worry about.

North of the Philippines and south of Taiwan the weather was still fine and I went across in the zed boat to inspect the tow. Everything was in order but climbing over the deck cargo of logs I slipped and dislocated my shoulder. It was agony. I had dislocated it once before in Hong Kong when climbing down the pilot ladder of our tow to Manila and had to be helped down. It had taken half an hour of painful manipulation by Ikan to get it back in and I did not go to the doctor. I tried to get it back in myself but was unsuccessful. I was filled with visions of being marooned on the tow for I could not get back into the zed boat. On this occasion the salvage crew with me came to my aid and on top of the logs – with much pain and lots of shouting – managed to get it back in. I was very relieved to climb back on board the tug.

We encountered rough weather up the coast of Taiwan and on to Japan but – the "Salvaliant" being a big, heavy tug – there were no problems when the "Runna" yawed out to one side or the other or stayed out on the beam.

It was cold in Japan when we delivered the tow to a small port in the inland sea and the "Salvaliant" had no heating only air-conditioning! No one spoke any English so I was glad our Japanese Selco representative turned up and we were able to get cold weather gear and some heaters.

The "Chenai Jayam" was a fully laden 50,000 ton bulk carrier and she broke down in the latitude of Hong Kong. I ran free at full speed in rough following weather to her location, and it was still rough when we connected the tow. The bulk carrier was a little big for the "Salvaliant", especially in the rough weather. The "Chenai Jayam" tended to yaw out to the beam and stay there, so progress was slow, but I was not worried – thinking it was a salvage. I was livid when I received a message informing me that it was a contract tow, and I sent some stroppy messages to Singapore about salvage.

'Have you enough fuel to reach Japan?' Signed Bond.

'Yes.' Signed Tew.

Later, when the slow progress was noticed,

'Can you reach Japan?' Signed Bond.

'Yes.' Signed Tew.

The weather became worse with a full gale blowing as we approached Japan with heavy seas. The seas were so large that the tow was almost out of sight at times and I took some good photographs. One I later sold to Nautical Publishing who published it in their book *This is Heavy Weather Sailing*.

We at last reached Shimonoseki where the "Chenai Jayam" anchored and we went into port. I was still very annoyed with the office for fixing a contract tow rather than a salvage tow, because neither the crew nor myself received a bonus for contracts and I felt very strongly that we should for dangerous and difficult pick-ups at sea – and told them so in messages.

Mr Koyanagi, the younger Selco representative in Tokyo, was there to meet the tug. He took me to a notary public – or the Japanese equivalent – and with much bowing and scraping, copies of my log showing the rough weather were notarised. The notary was an old man in traditional dress, and entering his office was like going back in time.

I received a message from the Indian owners of the "Chenai Jayam" that their representative on board the ship off Kobe had a bonus for myself and the crew if I cared to go and pick it up. I caught the Japanese fast train Shinkansen, commonly known as the Bullet, and went to Kobe. I was met by their agent and taken out to the ship and given $5,000 as a bonus for the crew. I felt more than justified in my stroppy messages to Selco, and I had never before heard of owners giving a cash bonus. My crew were more than happy when I arrived back on board the "Salvaliant" and gave them their bonus.

A few weeks later we ran free back to Hong Kong and I had a good moan at Marie Louise about bonuses which, no doubt, went straight back to her father, which was the intention!

We held some rather liquid curry lunches on board the tug in the harbour, the wine being served in good cut glass. They must have been successful because people came back a second time, and often lunch did not finish until 16:00 in the afternoon!

***

I was sent out on spec for a ship with an engine breakdown, but she got going again. However, instead of returning to Hong Kong, I was instructed to proceed to Singapore for dry docking.

William Crafter, or Bill to his friends, was installed in a minute office next to Mr K. Why EEK employed this man I did not discover until years later, and it certainly was not for his expertise. He was a retired major who, he said, had been on the staff of General, now Field Marshal, Carver.

Major Crafter was a big man with a rather high affected voice and he knew nothing about tugs and even less about salvage. He was apparently senior to Alan Bond and close to Mr K. His name had appeared on some of the replies to my stroppy messages. My moaning must have had its effect because there was talk of giving the crew a bonus, so I had to write a memo explaining I had already collected one from the owners.

I think Crafter decided to take me down a peg or two because he and Bond inspected the tug alongside in the yard. Bond, who was not given to writing memos, wrote a very shirty one to me complaining about the state of the tug, and in particular some grease nipples which were not working. I wrote back stating that Mr K had told me not to waste paint because the tug was going into dry dock on her return to Singapore. I pointed out that the nipples he complained about were been welded up on his, Mr Bond's instructions, and that is why they did not work. I copied Bond's memo and my reply to Mr K and that was the end of the matter!

Singapore Port Authority would only issue a port clearance valid for 24 hours and then it had to be renewed. They rejected the case for giving a salvage tug an open port clearance – which was the obvious thing to do – and if too many port clearances were issued without being used they objected. Typical bureaucrats following rules. I suggested to Mr Bond that when the tug was ready we should get a port clearance and sail, staying outside port limits. We would then beat the competition who were inside port limits; the gamble was which side of Singapore to stand by!

The refit was completed and the tug was fully stored for three months, including wine and beer.

I sailed and anchored outside port limits on the Western side of Singapore, technically in Malaysian waters.

'Proceed salvage speed to....' the given coordinates were north of Sumatra '... and assist "Sealift Mediterranean".' Signed Bond.

It was not long before we were running at just over fifteen knots up the calm Malacca Straits in bright sunshine expecting to be in charge of the salvage.

It was when we arrived I discovered a new employee of Selco was already on site and was the designated salvage master. I sent a very curt message back indeed and received one back from EEK.

'Get on with the salvage and will discuss on your return.'

The "Sealift Mediterranean" was the American equivalent of the British RFA, and the government were not pleased that one of their ships – a loaded tanker – had ripped open her bottom on a charted rock and was polluting the sea north of Indonesia. Only quick action by the master of a Selco tug operating in the vicinity had prevented the ship sinking. A full discharge of the cargo was made to a lightening tanker. Selco divers sealed the huge gash in the bottom, from the forepeak to 2 feet forward of the engine room. They worked surrounded by sharks. We took special precautions with rubbish, dumping it with a small tug at least five miles from the casualty.

The senior Americans used to come on board the "Salvaliant" for refreshments, which were not available on the dry American ship, and to watch the occasional erotic film. I discovered I was nicknamed The Duke by the Americans!

When the patching was finished I towed the "Sealift Mediterranean" to Singapore. The 'salvage master' stayed on board my tug overnight and the next morning I discovered that the fridge in the spare cabin, which had been full of beer, was empty. The salvage master could not be awoken. I was not only not pleased, I was incensed.

I had my meeting with Mr K, who apologised for the situation and said it was force of circumstances and not to worry – other opportunities would occur. I told him about the empty fridge and perhaps there was a problem. The man did not last long. He did not appear at the office for four days and Knobby Halls found him in his flat passed out surrounded by empty bottles. He was flown back to the UK.

***

Selco Shipyard built nine barges for Iran and they were to be towed as three tows three high. "Salvaliant" was designated to tow them and, after discussion, it was agreed to tow them one behind the other. The barges were stacked in the yard – the lashings welded – and they were towed out to the "Salvaliant" in Western Anchorage.

I put two of them alongside in the 69 position and one aft. Streaming the tow was tricky but successfully concluded, and the long tow to the Persian Gulf commenced. The weather was fine and the voyage uneventful. The most interesting bit was up the coast of India from Cape Comorin to Trivandrum, which I passed close to and wrote an article 'A Day on the Coast of India' which was published in the *Nautical Magazine*.

At the entrance to the river for Bandar Mashur, the Iranian port on the east side of the head of the Persian Gulf, there were a lot of ships at anchor. We waited with the barges strung out astern, expecting a long wait. Some of the ships had been waiting for many weeks. There was a certain amount of ship visiting, the weather being fine.

About a week later I received a message in the evening.

'Pilot boarding a.m.'

This was good news and the crew worked hard getting the tow ready. We put one tow on one side and one tow on the other, and the third tow astern because it was not possible to tow up river with all the barges astern – we would have been too long. As it was we were a pretty big 'ship' 400 feet long and 140 feet beam!

The next morning the pilot boat came over and the pilot said, "What speed can you make?"

"Oh, about eight knots," I replied.

"That's OK. Follow me, I am taking that ship up." He pointed to a loaded cargo ship. "I will be listening out on channel 16." And with that he departed.

"Jesus, heave up the anchor," I said, and, to Fernando, "Standby engines."

I got under way and headed to the fairway buoy, the crew checking the barges. The ship the pilot boarded overtook me and I increased to full speed, the tug steering normally balanced by the barges either side.

The Admiralty chart showed the river was buoyed all the way to Bandar Mahshahr and the surrounding banks were flat marshes. The ship with the pilot was pulling ahead, doing about fifteen knots. I called up on the VHF but there was no answer, and within the hour he had disappeared and I was on my own! It was a long way up the river but, having started, I was not turning back so continued. The tide was ebbing so my progress was slow over the land and as the water fell, so more of the banks were revealed. It was flat and featureless and I was very dependent on the buoys.

At dusk I anchored at the side of the channel but spent an uneasy night because the tug dragged. The next morning I arrived at the port and delivered the barges.

Three days later I received my clearance and the agent said that as I had come up the river without a pilot I could go down the river without one as well. Halfway down I anchored and took the lifeboat away to a barge up a creek I had seen on the upriver trip. It was aground but by dint of towing with the lifeboat, I got it afloat and towed it back to the tug and connected up. I sent a message to Selco informing them I had salved a barge and what would they like me to do with it. I continued on down the river.

'Anchor the barge and proceed Dubai for bunkers,' the instructions came back, which is what we did – leaving a light on it. I was very pleased with myself and crew.

I left Dubai for the Straits of Hormuz. On the way I passed a green wreck buoy with the word 'Dara' written on it and stopped the "Salvaliant" to pay my respects to the 238 dead. It evoked many memories of the disaster, not least my time in the water, the corpse, the imagined shark, and the burning inferno on B deck.

I continued on to Colombo where I went alongside the Yugoslav cargo ship "Volosko", which had engine problems and required towing to Singapore. The "Salvaliant" also suffered engine problems and the air-conditioning had packed up on the tug as well. It was hot in the port so I retired to the Oberoi Hotel, while the chief engineer and engine crew repaired the engine. The Oberoi is a spectacular hotel with a huge atrium, the rooms running off the surrounding balconies.

A week later – with the Yugoslavs leaping up and down with the delay – we were ready. The difficulty was to get the "Volosko" out of the narrow entrance. After discussions with the master attendant (harbour master in other ports) and Razzle Dazzle, the senior pilot, who had been fourth officer on the "Dara", I decided to tow her out with the "Salvaliant" on a very short tow with the two harbour tugs either side. It all went well, with Razzle on the "Volosko", and I towed her out of Colombo and on to Singapore. She yawed about all over the place, being even keel, but even though she was at times out on the beam, the tug behaved very well and I was able to steer at all times.

Nobody said anything about my stay in the Oberoi and the company paid the bill through the tug portage bill.

I gave evidence to Dennis Rixon who was living in a suite in the Goodwood Park Hotel, one of the most expensive and nicest hotels in Singapore. The food was very good and the beer expensive. However, there was a time limit on my stay in Singapore and he got on with the work – the poor secretary having to work overtime. There was a very jolly Sunday lunch with Mr K in the Hilton.

I ran free up to the Gulf, bunkered in Dubai and went alongside the "Majma Two", which had been moored on the Dubai Petroleum oil field for 20 years. Together with "Majma One", these tankers were the storage ships which held the crude pumped up from the oil field.

The engine room and accommodation had been cut off so they were completely square astern. The salvage association surveyor insisted that we tow the ships with 25,000 tons of ballast which seemed quite ridiculous. It would slow down the tow considerably and to my mind not make it any safer. Peter on the "Salvanquish" agreed and so did Bond in Singapore. As a safety precaution in case of leaks – for the ships were old, which was why they were going to Singapore for refit – we put portable pumps on deck.

Eventually we got under way and as soon as the oil field was out of sight, I sent my salvage crew across to the "Majma" and told them to pump out the ballast. Peter did the same with his and we increased the towing speed by a couple of knots. The "Salvanquish" was a considerably more powerful tug than the "Salvaliant" and towed the "Majma One" a lot faster. Peter was soon days ahead of me and got round Sri Lanka before the monsoon really broke.

One of the engines on the "Salvaliant" was sick. We rigged a sail on the main mast utilising hatch covers, which both increased the speed a little and steadied the tug in the beam weather. My crew objected saying if anyone saw us they would be humiliated but perked up when they realised the sail really did help. If you are only doing four knots, an increase of half a knot makes a big difference.

Eventually the starboard engine became so sick that it had to be stopped and could only be used in an emergency – the block was cracked. Speed was down to two and a half knots or so and obviously I was going to need help.

The South West monsoon had broken with its strong winds and rain. That was fine for Peter already round Sri Lanka, it gave him a fair wind.

'Proceed Amani Island and assist "Pacifico Everrett".'

The originator of the message seemed to have forgotten that I was towing a 40,000 ton storage tanker and had engine problems! It was the days before satellite navigators or GPS and I had not obtained sun sights for days, I posted lookouts up the mast and on the monkey island and we found the island in heavy rain. It was a relief. It was much too deep to anchor, so I steamed up and down in the lee of the low palm-treed island.

The casualty was on the other side of the island, the windward side and the only way to reach her was with the rubber zed boat across the lagoon. The problem was getting into the lagoon. We discovered the entrance was at the northern end of the island but the seas were breaking across it. I took the zed boat away with the two divers and the fitter Eusebio leaving my tug and tow in charge of the chief officer Edgar. We stood by off the reef entrance and watched and a pattern emerged when there were no breaking waves. After conferring and obtaining agreement from the three crew with me we decided to give it a go. Picking the right moment I increased to full speed and made for the entrance and as we entered a wave rose up behind us and seemed to chase us in, breaking just behind the rubber boat. We would have been dead if it had swamped us and thrown us onto the reef.

Laughing with relief we made it over the lagoon with Elmo the diver standing in the bow directing, showing me where the coral heads were. We made it safely to where the "Pacifico Everett" was aground high and almost dry on the reef with waves breaking over her. I anchored our boat and we waded towards the edge of the reef and the side of the ship. I slipped and found myself being swept towards the stern of the ship where the waves were breaking and I knew I would be swept into the surf and certain unpleasant death. Romeo Eusebio saw what was happening and somehow caught hold of my arm and pulled me to my feet saving me. We eventually climbed onboard via a pilot ladder.

After my inspection and the report of the divers who sounded round and Eusebio who sounded the tanks I knew she was finished there was no way we could salve her. The Pacifico Everrett was scrap.

We made our way back across the lagoon and realised we could not get out through the continuously breaking channel seas. We went ashore and carried the boat across the island meeting some people who offered to help us. I asked them who they were and they said "we are lepers" and to my eternal shame I dropped the boat and with my three crew we ran into the water. The lepers fell about laughing and told us they were not infectious and we would not catch anything from them. Apologising we came back and together carried the boat to a safe launch place and crossed the reef back to the "Salvaliant" towing the huge "Majma."

It was with considerable relief I climbed onboard, showered, sank a cold beer and composed my message to Singapore. In reply to my query concerning the lepers the message simply said "don't touch." They were sending Peter with the

"Salvanquish," which had reached Singapore safely to assist. Various suggestions were made for salvage but none were practical.

***

The "Salvanquish" duly arrived some days later together with the P and I club surveyor who declared the ship a total loss. With agreement from local administrator who was visiting the island we landed the crew of the casualty and they were ferried out to the "Salvaliant" in an island rowing boat. We took them to Cochin after handing over the tow to the "Salvanquish" Peter throwing an empty can of beer over the side as he pulled away.

We were three weeks in Cochin. Knobby Halls was more than welcome when he turned up – very supportive and a convivial companion. He managed to weld up the engine and departed with the sick AB back to Singapore.

I lived in the Malabar Hotel, which was on the island in the middle of the harbour, and the agent came for drinks every night. It was all very Indian and gentlemanly, and the hotel was something out of the 1930s.

I visited the synagogue centre of the oldest Jewish community in India – dwindling in numbers – and the grave of Vasco de Gama.

All our cholera immunisations were out of date and the health authorities insisted that we all be injected. The female doctor turned up with an old-fashioned syringe and needle and even more old-fashioned ideas of hygiene. When I suggested that the needle might be disinfected, she told me not to be fussy; and when I remonstrated at the use of the same needle for everyone she told me no injections, no certificate, no port clearance. I submitted.

***

I sailed out into the South West monsoon with instructions to proceed to the Somali coast. It was rough and the "Salvaliant" pitched heavily, shipping seas, and rolled. One of the divers was so seasick I though he was going to die on me. He could not hold down anything and became severely dehydrated. In the end he was slipping in and out of consciousness. When we reached the coast and the sea calmed down he miraculously recovered, within a couple of hours he was eating and back to normal.

I found the "Universal King" anchored off the shore about fifty miles north of Mogadishu. The north-bound current was running at about seven knots and I wondered how I was going to tow this loaded ship against the current to the port. The sun was shining, which was welcome after the rain at sea during the crossing from India.

There was a huge amount of salvage experience amongst the crew, especially the bosun and Paquito, the diver, and the officers. After discussion I anchored ahead of the ship and dropped back, putting the stern alongside the anchor cable – ever mindful of my vulnerable propeller. The bosun shackled a strop round the chain and the main tow wire to the strop.

I steamed ahead, picking up our anchor. I had to steam at seven knots through the water just to remain stationary over the land, and the second engine was clutched in before the anchor was up. Speed was slowly increased, the strop ran down the anchor chain of the "Universal King" until it snagged on the anchor and when enough power had been put on, the anchor lifted off the bottom and I had the tow under control at seven knots through the water. With full power we only made just under eight knots and took almost two days to reach Mogadishu.

The port was not yet open, although built, so the tow had to be anchored in the stream in the strong current. When in position I slowed down, slacking out the tow wire; the anchor went on the bottom, anchoring the "Universal King". The anchor of the "Salvaliant" was let go and I dropped back alongside the cable. The tow wire was heaved up the tight chain and the strop came back up to the surface of the water where it was unshackled.

The "Salvaliant" was leaking like a sieve through the stern gland. There was a dredger in the port and I made contact with the master asking him if there was enough water for me to come in. When he replied in the affirmative I asked him to help me get permission to come in, he obviously knew the harbour master. Permission was granted, the harbour master came on board and drank all my Mateus Rose wine with me while the divers repacked the stern gland.

The harbour master was a cheerful fellow. He told me not to go outside the port unless I was in a taxi if I valued my life; the Filipinos would be safe enough. The agent, who was the agent for the "Universal King", was not really interested in us.

I went by taxi to the best hotel and spent many hours trying to get through on the telephone to Singapore. I eventually talked to Alan Bond and he agreed, when I had got my termination letter signed, I should proceed to Mombasa for repairs. There was nothing in Mogadishu except dust, heat and rather thin people. When the the Mateus Rose ran out the harbour master said we had to go but luckily I had the termination letter by then.

Mombasa was a welcome change, although it had gone downhill since independence. I had a run-in with a Kenyan customs man about the beer and wine in my fridge – used for entertaining – and it took a hefty bribe to keep me out of trouble! He threatened to have me beaten to a pulp.

Knobby turned up again and looked after the repairs and dry docking. I was using a hotel for sending messages to Singapore until I realised it was owned by the Italian salvor Murri Frere. I changed hotels!

I called on and made friends with Peter Philips, who owned another salvage company, I thought the connection might be useful to Selco. Peter was very hospitable and owned a beautiful house on the mainland overlooking the back of Mombasa.

I hired a dinghy and sailed in Mombasa harbour. Knobby and I stayed in the Oceanic Hotel overlooking the entrance to Mombasa.

Shortly after Knobby left to go back to Singapore, I received instructions to sail for Saldanha Bay in South Africa. I had not been feeling very well in Mombasa and was almost seasick when we cleared the reef at the entrance and hit the ocean swell.

Europa Island, in the Madagascar Channel, has no port and

its only inhabitants are a few meteorologists and seagulls. I was instructed to look for a fishing boat that had run aground, and steamed round the island to find her. She was high and dry above the surf line on the windward side, great rollers beating down on the reef and throwing spray high into the air. My crew were apprehensive at being so close and so was I if truth be told.

I anchored on the reef in the lee of the island, with the stern kept clear by the offshore wind. I was feeling distinctly seedy so sent Edgar off with a salvage crew to make their way overland to the fishing boat.

They had a lovely time with the friendly meteorologists, who drove them across the island on a tractor. The birdlife was so dense that some were crushed by the wheels.

Edgar reported they boarded the fishing boat but she was a write-off. A feast of seagulls' eggs was eaten, the anchor was heaved up and I proceeded on our way – the crew, who had overindulged in the rich eggs, lost them when the ocean swell was felt.

"I am a European Englishman." I concluded on my arrival message to the agents, Ellerman Lines in South Africa. So many people in new ports came on board concluding that Captain Tew from Singapore must be Chinese or Asian. I did not want any confusion in apartheid South Africa.

***

ILL

I cleared in at Capetown. The doctor came on board to minister to the 70 per cent of the crew who had caught 'something' from their beautiful, silk-skinned, Somali girlfriends. When leaving the port I was sick over the pilot's feet; he was not very impressed. I was feeling distinctly ill and contemplated going to the doctor. However, in Saldanha Bay, which was north of Capetown, I felt a little better and started preparing for the long tow to the Persian Gulf. The "Salvaliant" was contracted to tow a dredge.

I was feeling ill again and plucking up courage to go and see the doctor, when someone turned up and told me that a ship was in trouble south of the Cape of Good Hope. It was cold and dismal weather but I perked up at the prospect of salvage and made preparations to leave. I phoned Singapore and Alan Bond agreed I should leave on spec and he would investigate the rumour. It would be a coup for Selco to perform a salvage on the coast of South Africa.

I steamed out of the harbour and ran down the rocky coast past Capetown. There was, indeed, a ship in trouble, but so was I. I was feeling very ill and I stopped eating, not able to hold anything down.

Once south of the Cape, the "Salvaliant" was almost in the Roaring Forties – the Westerlies that sweep round the world causing huge seas in bad weather. Tasmania, off the Australian coast, was the next stop to the east; and Tierra Del Fuego, in South America, to the west.

The "Ville de Mahebourg" was, without a rudder, heading towards Antarctica, holding her bow up into the weather. I raced south at maximum speed – the old girl running in the cold water at over fifteen knots – swooping and dancing over the swells, or so it seemed to me. Five hundred miles off the Cape of Good Hope, deep into the Southern Ocean – the sky overcast, the sea grey – I came up on the "Ville de Mahebourg" slowly making way towards the South Pole.

"Do you agree Lloyd's Open Form?" I asked the master on the VHF.

"Oui, yes," came back the reply.

That was sufficient. I had a contract, I had an LOF in the Southern Ocean. I was elated, a Selco first; Mr K would be pleased, even Mr Bond would be pleased and I would have one up on Captain Hancox! I just had to be successful. I was feeling so ill I could barely stand up, and had not eaten since leaving Saldanha Bay.

The master of the casualty did not want to stop for fear of rolling too heavily when he swung beam onto the huge swell, but I told him he would have to when I connected. I told him I would be as quick as possible and it was up to him to heave in the towing gear fast.

I climbed heavily up onto the monkey island and told Edgar to come up with a chair and stay with me; Loreto, the second mate, should man the radio. I felt sick and dizzy but I was determined to connect and tow the "Ville de Mahebourg" to safety.

The tug was shipping heavy seas on the tow deck. Tough, dependable Javier Patani, the bosun, and wild Paquito Delos Reyes, the diver, were standing by on the after hatch – with the crew looking at me and then the rolling and pitching casualty. It was getting dark, the sky was leaden and gloomy and I had to get a move on. I decided to take a risk, I knew I could depend on my crew and I guessed I could depend on the French; it was whether I lasted out sitting in my chair, braced against the movement of the tug.

I crossed the bow of the now drifting ship and a heaving line thudded onto the tow deck. In a trice it was made fast to the polypropylene line and with the French heaving like mad men, it flew out over the side and up onto the "Ville de Mahebourg". I gave a kick ahead on the engine – turning the tug parallel to the casualty – the propeller away from the line. The wire pendant slid over the well greased gunwale, followed by the stretcher. The tug was very close to the ship and the wire pendant disappeared through the fairlead on the forecastle of the casualty.

Shortly afterwards the French signalled they had made fast. There were cheers from my tug and the tow and I steamed ahead, paying out the tow wire to almost its maximum length. I needed the catenary in the heavy swell.

I increased speed, turned north and when the French told me they had backed up the bitts on which we were towing, I increased to maximum power. The "Ville de Mahebourg" went out on one side and stayed there. We made good speed.

I catnapped in the captain's chair on the bridge, feeling very ill indeed. The connection had taken it out of me and I was having difficulty holding down any liquids, so was becoming dehydrated and at times hallucinating.

I perked up a bit four days later when I saw Table Mountain, the flat plateau above Capetown, dominating the city capped by cloud. It was cold and started to rain when the pilot and tugs came out. I insisted on remaining connected and towed the casualty on short tow to the berth, assisted by the harbour tugs. Once the crew disconnected and recovered the towing gear – their wet weather gear dripping with water – I wearily climbed on board the "Ville de Mahebourg". The captain signed my termination letter, offered me refreshment, which I refused, and I returned to the tug almost at the end of my tether.

I sailed shortly afterwards for Saldanha Bay and let Edgar take charge, retiring to my bunk. I managed to be on the bridge entering Saldanha Bay and, once alongside, I took a taxi to the local hotel and went to bed. The doctor was called and he diagnosed jaundice and wanted to put me in hospital there and then. I refused until a relief turned up. I phoned Alan Bond in Singapore and told him I was sick and please send a relief.

Edgar turned up for instructions, coming into my bedroom. The wife of the owner said that he could not stay, he would have to stand in the corridor because he was black. I lost my temper, shouted at her to call the police; Edgar was staying and he was worth a hundred people like her. She retired hurt but I had no more nonsense. Various crew turned up to wish me well and told me how much fun they were having in South Africa.

Ebullient, intense, talkative Hughie Murray turned up from Singapore. He was a retired commander from the Navy and mad as a hatter; a bit like a bull in a china shop. He got things done, was intelligent but trod on toes. I was exceedingly glad to see his large figure and departed in an ambulance to hospital in Capetown. Two months later I flew back to England.

"What were the riots like, I was worried?" my mother asked.

"What riots, Mum?"

Amazing how the Press distort the news.

I spent a couple of months in England recuperating but my mother does not pretend to be a good nurse. If you are sick go to bed, if not then you are well!

I stayed at Thorns Beach, which is a marvellous place to convalesce with the ever-changing view out of the window. Now that we had the freehold – which I had paid for – there was a permanence which, when it had been leasehold, was missing. There was no 'one day it has to be handed back'.

The only cloud on the horizon was the coastal erosion, and steadily each year a little piece more of the bank along the beach was washed away. My salvage life seemed utterly remote from the peace and quiet at Thorns and the birdlife at low water.

I gave my "Ville de Mahebourg" evidence to Dennis Rixon in London. Robert Elbourne, as ebullient as ever, and all the people I had worked with were pleased to see me. Richard Shaw had left to set up his own firm. The daggy pub across the road was no better and Corvinos had not changed.

SINGAPORE

Singapore was as hot and sticky as ever when I arrived back, and I stayed in the Orchid Inn. The "Salvaliant" was not back from the gulf and her long tow. I went out with Mr K a few times but was strictly 'on the wagon' after my jaundice.

The "Citta di Savona" had a collision in Singapore Eastern Anchorage one evening and was pouring crude into the harbour Selco salvage vessel "Salvista" reported. I was in the office and immediately went over the road and boarded the fast crew boat "Salvital." An hour later I was onboard the casualty but the master refused to sign my LOF. I finally persuaded him and set to work. Selco divers were soon on site, lots of small tugs, the `Selco oil barge, the "Salvital", the "Salvirile" and an oil boom. The Singapore Port Authority were there with their fire tugs, launches with surveyors, and old Uncle Tom Cobley and all! Amidst all the activity the master said his owners instructed him he was not to sign the LOF but it was already onboard the "Salvista." However he seemed quite happy to let us get on with the salvage, glad I was now responsible for salving his ship.

The general chaos got sorted out, the divers plugged the leak, cargo was transferred to another tank to reduce the level of oil to below the damage and – by daylight – all was under control. The captain offered me a beer and I thought to myself if I am fit enough to perform salvage operations I am fit enough to have a beer. He signed my termination letter and I departed well pleased with myself. A signed Lloyds Open Form within Singapore port limits and signed by me.

Selco kept very good connections in Djakarta, which were essential if you wanted to work in corrupt Indonesia. I flew down to Djakarta, the flat land criss-crossed with canals very visible from the air, and a hot nightlife reminiscent of Holland and Amsterdam.

Mr Soekardono met me at the airport and took me to his

office, where arrangements were made for me to go out to the ship aground on a reef some fifty miles from Tanjong Priok. Tugs and barges were on the way from Singapore. I thought it a good idea to take one of his office staff with me as an interpreter, and he proved very useful dealing with the Indonesian master and the various officials who turned up. He and I went out on a chartered tug after a good dinner.

The Selco fleet arrived. I laid ground tackle, discharged enough cargo to refloat, and took the ship to Tanjong Priok where the cargo was reloaded from the Selco barges. It was even hotter and stickier than Singapore!

Selco purchased a burnt out passenger ship that was aground off Port Klang for scrap. Alan Bond told me to go and bring her down to Singapore – the "Salvanquish" was on the way from Madagascar. The "Salvirile" with Juanito Ventua, the ex-chief officer of the "Salviper", in command was alongside. It turned out to be a bit more difficult than it sounded. The ex "Cambodge" was heavily aground, with a 15 degree list and partly flooded.

I lived ashore in hot and steamy Port Klang, going out each day with the divers in a chartered launch. The ship was sealed and the water pumped out. Juanito was such a good salvor, an excellent organiser, that I was almost superfluous.

One Sunday William Crafter arrived on the scene to look at the ship. I could not believe my eyes when this apparition arrived wearing white trousers and white shoes – white shoes to visit a salvage operation on a dead, burnt out, listing passenger ship!

I took him out in the launch and he carefully climbed aboard the tug, refusing a cold drink in the captain's cabin with Juanito. I suggested he might look around the Selco-owned passenger ship but he took one look at the gangway plank, looked at his spotless white shoes, looked at the oily deck on the passenger ship and declined. I took him ashore and wondered why on earth Mr K employed this retired army major.

After the episode of the nipples I had written to Edward, who was a major with the Royal Engineers, and asked him to find out more about Major Crafter. It turned out he had been in the commissariat and, far from retiring, he had resigned from the army rather than face a court martial for having his finger in the till. White shoes, I ask you!

The "Salvanquish" arrived with a very odd master. Still, I could not complain, he did what I told him to. We refloated the ship and sitting in the crow's nest on the foremast of the "Cambodge" with a couple of cold beers, I piloted her out through the narrow channel, with the "Salvanquish" towing and the "Salvirile" astern. We just made it to the Malacca Straits before dark, and I stayed on the tow to Singapore.

It was eerie on the burnt out passenger ship as she silently moved through the black water completely dark, the ghosts of personnel on the way to French Indo China (later Vietnam) easily imagined, apprehensive perhaps on the outward voyage, joyous on the homeward. All finished after the fall of Saigon to the communists, masterminded by a French educated man.

I anchored her just outside Singapore port limits.

UNIQUE MARINER

I was back in command of the "Salvaliant" which was alongside the ex "Cambodge" and the salvage crew were removing the engine stores, or those that Knobby wanted. I was not too interested and it was exceedingly hot and oily down in the engine room and shaft tunnel.

I was on the bridge of the "Salvaliant" idly enjoying the fresh air and keeping a lookout for anything untoward, as any good salvor should. I noticed in the distance a ship, which appeared to be stopped or at anchor in Indonesian waters. A bit unusual, perhaps an engine problem I thought. It was a fine day and I continued to watch the world's shipping entering or leaving the Malacca Straits.

Some time later the ship I had seen was still there and definitely stopped. I took a bearing from the wing gyro repeater and laid it off on the chart. Yes, right through Selco treasure island Nipa Shoal.

My heart beat faster, and the adrenalin started to flow as I shouted, "Action stations, we are leaving!"

My crew thought I had gone mad until I shouted, "Ship aground!"

The engines were started in record time, the salvage crew discharging the stores dropped what they were carrying, shouted to the men below and came running on board.

"Cut the lines," I ordered from the monkey island control position, ringing double full ahead on the telegraph.

The "Salvaliant" took off like a scalded cat, the water bubbling under the stern scraping down the side of the "Cambodge", and literally flew the few miles to Nipa Shoal. I don't know what Fernando did to the engines, but the old tug had never been so fast in her life.

"Swing out the zed boat ready for launching," I told Edgar, "and then standby here with me."

Off the grounded ship I stopped, handed over to Edgar and

went quickly to the zed boat. I had maintained radio silence, not wanting to alert the competition.

Paquito drove the zed boat and together with a couple of salvage crew, we sped over to the "Unique Mariner", whose name I could see on the stern. There was a pilot ladder over the side, so I climbed on board, Lloyd's Form in my pocket, and told the man on deck to take me to his captain.

I was received by the Taiwanese captain and his chief officer in the captain's cabin. After a few pleasantries I offered to refloat him on Lloyd's Open Form, which I showed him. He agreed and we signed.

I was elated and on cloud nine as I went back to the tug, and the crew gave a cheer when I waved the LOF. I sent the salvage crew back to the casualty with the pelican hook and told Ops I was salving a ship on LOF and was about to connect and please organise Indonesian permits.

The anchor was being weighed when I received a message over the Motorola radio from my second officer who was on the casualty waiting to connect. The master wanted to see me immediately and we were not to connect. My heart sank, what had gone wrong? I went over in the zed boat.

The master wanted the Lloyds Form back. He could not have it back. Another tug was coming to tow him off. I argued that I was there first and all ready to connect. He offered me US$500 – tea money – if I would give him the form back. I was shocked and insulted to be offered a bribe and told him so. He told me to take back any gear we had put on board his ship. I had no option but to comply with the instructions of the master and reluctantly gave the order and departed. My Lloyds Form was still until the master 'terminated' the contract which he had not done, merely asked for it back. I returned to the tug most disgruntled and informed Ops.

And so the "Salvaliant" entered the English law books and I ended up in front of the Admiralty judge Henry Brandon, now Lord Brandon.

The learned judge said, "This is a most interesting case. If I find against Captain Tew he is guilty of fraud, perhaps criminal fraud; if I find against the master of the "Unique

Mariner" he has merely made a mistake."

Food for thought, I could end up in jail!

It is a daunting experience to be a witness in court, especially when accused of doing something I had not done. The master of the "Unique Mariner" stated under oath, backed up by his chief officer, that I had come on board his ship and said, "I am from the agents, sign here." He had been expecting a tug sent by the agent, whom he had signalled that he was aground.

I denied I said any such thing. I was in the witness box for six hours, most of it being cross-examined by David Steele QC, a long nosed, supercilious Old Etonian. He started asking me questions of detail which I could not remember, so I turned to the judge and said,

"Your Honour, if I could have my log book I could answer that question."

"I don't see why Captain Tew cannot have his log book," said the learned judge.

I was made up. I got my log and any other document I asked for and answered all Mr Steele's questions satisfactorily.

The judge found for Selco. The case is the precedent on the most important question of the authority of a master to sign a Lloyd's Form. (He can.)

Selco claimed compensation as a dispossessed salvor and won that case too, being paid what would have been paid if the salvage had been successfully carried out by me.

BARGE PASTEE COLOMBO

I flew to Bahrain and took command of the "Salvanquish". She was very different from the "Salvaliant" being single engined and more powerful, thus more easy to manoeuvre. There were problems starting the engine but it normally went after a few tries. Compressed air was required to turn and start the engine and like the "Salvaliant" big ship style, if you wanted the propeller to stop, the engine had to be stopped. Once the engine was running it kept going.

I left Bahrain bound for Singapore running free. I had to stop on passage off Muscat, where the "Dara" should have been when the bomb went off, for engine repairs. After the repairs were finished the chief had a lot of difficulty restarting the engine. I informed the office and was ordered to Bombay. Knobby turned up and we went to see the harbour master and obtained permission to enter the docks so the engine could be immobilised for repairs. One week later, with the engine apparently working, I left – bound for Singapore and salvage standby. It had been a pleasant stay in Bombay, living in the Taj Mahal Hotel and doing a few sightseeing tours.

The weather was foul being the south west monsoon, rain, wind, humidity but the crew all perked up when we were ordered to Colombo and assist the "Salvigilant" with the salvage of the barge "Pastee."

Aitken Spence were our agents in Colombo and the "Salvanquish" was looked after by Michael Mack and Nimal Maralande. We were given a nice berth near the city and Michael, who had taken me to see the Master Attendant whom I had met over the "Volosko" tow. He arranged for an open-dated port clearance and permission to sail without a pilot in an emergency, provided we paid for him.

The " "Salvigilant" came alongside us and the master came onboard to give me his report and quite a saga it had been. He tried to tow her off three weeks previously and got himself into trouble with the towing line around his propellors, anchored on a lee shore with his stern just clear of the breakers on the reef. Divers sent by the agent managed to clear one propellor and he returned to Colombo and had not been out since.

The barge "Pastee", loaded with sawn timber, was aground off Bambalapitiya railway station and I went to have a look with the divers and master of the "Salvigilant." She appeared to be salvable so I told Singapore and they ordered me to do so. The South West monsoon was breaking, it had broken further north, so speed was of the essence if we were to be successful.

I made a mistake, she was a lot harder aground than I thought and the divers could not get at the holes in the bottom to patch. I moved the "Salvanquish" to an even better berth in the port and after a lot of meetings and guarantees to the customs, discharged all the salvage gear from the tug and trucked it up to the railway station.

The barge was aground on rocks close to the shore, which was a bank about 6 feet high. A few yards inland was a 20 feet high wall protecting the railway station. Behind the wall were the platforms and railway lines. I obtained permission to cross the railway lines with my gear from the railway authorities, which was done with Michael's assistance.

We set up shop behind the wall on the bank, with the large compressor to drive the air pumps and pump air into the barge, the generator to run the electric submersibles pumps and other bits and pieces. It was hot and humid and a swell was running in, causing the barge to move about on the rocks.

When all was ready, pumps on board, air pumped into the accessible tanks, the "Salvigilant" came round to tow off the barge. The master anchored her off, the divers made the towing connection, there was a good swell running, and I instructed him to commence towing. He picked up the anchor and swung the tug from side to side at full power. Apart from a few grinding noises nothing happened. The "Pastee" should have come off but she did not and we concluded she must be impaled on a rock. The "Salvigilant" returned to Colombo.

After discussion with my salvage crew and Edgar, Michael took me to an engineering works where I had a tripod made. With the equipment from the "Salvanquish" we rigged up a breeches buoy system to discharge the cargo of sawn timber. There was an odd feeling in Colombo, a sense of foreboding, an uneasiness I had not experienced before; a bit like continually looking over your shoulder on a dark night for the non-existent stalker – fear. The barge and our activities were attracting a lot of interest and timber was a valuable commodity in Sri Lanka.

The crew and officers from the two tugs and myself started to discharge the timber and truck it away to a warehouse but it was slow work. The occasional plank was lost, drifting ashore on the Colombo side of the railway station where a crowd had gathered. They eagerly looted the timber.

This went on for a few days with the crowd picking up the planks lost overboard increasing to about four hundred. Through Michael I was employing a gang of Sri Lankans to assist in the discharge.

***

The mood in Colombo had become tense, something was going to happen. One morning there were shouts and screams behind the wall and then the rhythmic thud of flesh being hit just like beating a steak.

Early in the afternoon I noticed the noise had stopped but I was in trouble myself. Quite a lot of timber had been washed off the barge and the gang on the Colombo side of the railway station were becoming very bold and had advanced almost to our camp. My Filipinos and Sri Lankans, totalling just over a hundred, were becoming increasingly agitated. I was standing on the bank, the two gangs either side of me, the barge to seaward and the wall behind my back. Suddenly a stone whizzed past my head from the looting gang. Another flew back from my gang. I was in the middle. I looked at the looters and saw in their faces something I had not seen before – a lust – the face on a fighter.

One of my Filipino divers ran up and said, "Come back, Cap, it's not safe," and ran back to our side.

But I knew I could not move. Stones were flying past me in increasing numbers and I realised I was in deep trouble. It was the beginning of a fight. The looters advanced, my gang advanced. I knew that as soon as blood was drawn there would be a full scale riot – the eyes in the faces of both sides had a glazed look, blood lust.

I could not run myself, even if I wanted to, with the wall on one side and the sea on the other. If I moved back to my side it would be a signal of weakness and the looters would attack. I felt quite calm but incredibly tense. I knew my life hung in the balance and it was by my own actions if I lived or died.

I was wearing white cotton working gloves. I put my hands in the air and, facing the looting gang, I shouted, "Stop! Stop I say." And then half turned and shouted to my side, "Fetch the police."

"Stop! Stop I say." I continued to face the looters with my hands in the air like a traffic warden stopping the traffic.

My side stopped throwing stones and then miraculously the looters stopped. The police arrived and the looters dissipated and vanished into thin air, leaving on the platform the remains of a man they had beaten to death with iron bars – the noise I had heard in the morning.

"That's it," I said to Edgar, "we are abandoning. Collect up the gear."

I retired to the local hotel for a calming drink or two and rang Michael Mack. He sent down the lorry with a crane and we cleared the site before dark. That night the riots started and over the next few days hundreds were killed. I took up residence in the Oberoi Hotel with a special curfew pass.

The riots were over in ten days.

A ship loaded with cement sank in the harbour and I took the "Salvanquish" alongside intending to salve her, but I did not have a contract. I experienced a lot of trouble manoeuvring the tug, the engine start problem had reoccurred.

My divers found the leak, patched it, and I started to pump out, lifting her off the bottom. A message from Selco told me not to raise her because we still did not have a contract. So I refilled the deep tank and put her back into the mud.

I was living in the Intercontinental, having moved from the Oberoi to be closer to the port. Some days later a Smit tug steamed into the harbour, came alongside the casualty and Reiner Castle boarded. He was their salvage master from Singapore. He informed me they had the contract to salve the sunken ship. I did not believe him, told him so, and said to do nothing until I returned.

I rushed ashore and phoned Singapore from the hotel. Mr K told me to hand over to Smits. I was incandescent with rage. London was open and I rang Ray Clarke to get the P&I club number. I rang Graham Edmiston, who had been one of Daiquiri's crew on the "Fastnet", and told him I could not believe what had happened. He said their Hong Kong office were handling the case and he would find out. He rang back later and told me he was sorry, he could not reverse the decision but he would be holding an enquiry.

I returned on board and handed over to Reiner, telling my crew to recover our gear. There were even more problems with the "Salvanquish" engine and I arrived back in the hotel in a very grim mood – unreliable tug, failure with the "Pastee" and now the loss of my salvage to Smits.

Alan Bond told me to bring the tug back to Singapore for repairs if I could get the engine to start. I moored the tug on the 'T' of the jetty opposite the entrance to the port near the dry dock, with light lines, the bow heading for the entrance. If the engine started I would steam straight out of the harbour and not stop until Singapore.

The Master Attendant agreed it was an emergency so did not need a pilot, provided we paid for him. It was morning time and a fine day in the South West monsoon. There was a heavy swell outside the breakwaters.

After 20 attempts the chief engineer ran out of compressed air and we waited until the bottles were all fully charged. He came up onto the monkey island and said he thought we should make repairs in Colombo. I persuaded him to have another go and after another 25 attempts, my nerve broke as well. I warped the tug back alongside the wharf and signalled Singapore. Knobby flew to Colombo and we dry docked the tug in the dock nearby. Knobby finally solved the starting problem.

STATESMAN / SALVANGUARD

I was home on leave and spent it sailing with my mother in "Mary Helen" through the Dutch canals, inside the German Frisian up the Elbe, through the Kiel Canal into the Baltic and so to Denmark for the World 420 Championships where James my youngest brother sailed for England. My mother was president of the 420 association. There was only one way through the canals with the yacht's fixed mast and the railway bridge in Amsterdam starting to close on us. The bridge is only open for ten minutes at midnight and we were late because of the engine. We called on Peter Lankester who was master of a new tug, the "Happy Hunter", and he took us out to his house near Utrecht.

We were 35 days in the canals and it rained on every one of them! My mother wrote up the cruise for the RCC Journal and it was published in *Roving Commissions*.

Selco, or more correctly Mr K, purchased the "Statesman" from United Towing. Although I did not know it at the time, Knobby recommended me to Bond as the best person to take over the tug, I always thought it was entirely on my own merits! Just goes to show what a good friend Knobby has been over the years. I was back in England and went up to Hull with him for the takeover.

It was an interesting business. The tug of Icelandic Cod War fame was laid up so we had to start from scratch. We hired a United Towing chief engineer who knew the tug to show us the ropes and teach Legaspi, who was to be the chief engineer. Roger Sario, ex "Salviper", was to be chief officer.

There was a strike in Hull and we were frightened we were going to be held up in the docks. Knobby and I got a scratch crew together, which included my brother Donald, and we sailed the tug to Southampton. It felt strange to be in command of a 'super' tug in the North Sea steaming south with the coast of England to starboard, across the Thames estuary and into the English Channel, in through Spithead and so to Southampton. The trip went well but no salvage, much to everyone's disappointment!

The "Salvanguard" – as Selco christened the tug – was refitted and a lot of salvage gear put on board, mostly bought through Frank of Interworld who owned the business in Alton, Hampshire. He was a retired naval petty officer who knew ships and it was a pleasure to deal with him. Telex over radio was fitted and I think we were the first commercial tug to be so fitted. It meant we could send and receive messages without anyone else monitoring them. There was only one radio station Berne in Switzerland which we could use. It turned out to be a real boon. It was a fully fitted out salvage super tug that left Southampton under Selco colours, the Singapore flag flying proudly from the gaff on the aftermast.

We enjoyed a good passage to Port Said but with no excitement. In Port Said our 'private' agent was Port Said Navigation and Shipping and I met the irrepressible, cheerful, hardworking Sayeed Hassan, who was the ultimate Egyptian Mr Fixit. He got things done in a country where mañana and 'tomorrow' are a way of life.

It was an uneventful, trouble-free passage through the Suez Canal and I gazed hungrily at the scrap ships anchored in the Bitter Lakes – the trapped ships of the war with Israel.

It was hot with a fair wind down the Gulf of Suez, the barren desert on one side and hills on the other. Although only a couple of hundred miles south of the Mediterranean, the climate was totally different from the northern winter. I stopped off at an old wreck aground halfway down on the Egyptian shore, but she was unsalvable and had been there a long time.

A small ship was stopped near the bottom end of the gulf. I plotted the radar bearing and distance and found she was aground on a reef.

"Action stations!" I shouted to galvanise the crew from their afternoon torpor. "Ship aground," I announced on the internal tannoy system.

The zed boat was made ready and I lay off close to and went

across. The "Mare" was a Turkish coaster loaded with canned goods bound for Aden. The captain was only too pleased to sign my Lloyd's Form and hugged and kissed me on both cheeks. I telexed Selco with the good news.

The divers' survey indicated that she was heavily aground, which confirmed she ran aground at full speed. I needed to be careful with my big tug, it was no use connecting up and ripping the coaster off if she left half her bottom behind on the reef. I needed to jettison some of the cargo and told Singapore. Unfortunately, the draught of the tug was too deep to allow me to go alongside, otherwise I would have used the tug as a barge. There was no alternative but to throw the canned goods on to the reef.

'Jettison as little cargo as possible to preserve values.' Signed EEK read the telex; the chairman as always the businessman.

The next day we connected up the tug and easily refloated the "Mare". The master signed my termination letter and again gave me a hug and kisses. We both proceeded south.

***

The next day, in the Red Sea, I heard on the VHF channel 16:

" "Salvanguard"! "Salvanguard"! Help, help, I am being attacked!"

I wondered what on earth had happened. The weather was reasonably good so I steamed up to the now stopped "Mare" and went across in the zed boat with my burliest crew armed with knives and crowbars. The crew were, indeed, engaged in a fight but stopped when we appeared over the rail. My crew kept close to me when I went on the bridge to find the master, who was effusive in his thanks. He said they had run out of food and could I supply him with any. And would I guide him to Aden, his compass was not very good.

"No problem at all if you sign here," I said, proffering a new LOF.

He signed with alacrity so I had a second Lloyd's Form on the same ship!

We sent across some food and I left two of my crew with a

Selco radio for the voyage to Aden. Shortly after telexing Singapore with the news of my second Lloyd's Form, I received a message to proceed to Jeddah and leave the "Mare" outside port limits.

After bunkering I continued on to Aden with the "Mare" following and there were no more incidents. Outside port limits I took off my crew and anchored while the "Mare" entered. Shortly afterwards I was called up by the Port Control and told to enter the port myself. Aden was communist and trouble and I had no intention of going in.

"Pick up the anchor, Roger," I instructed the chief officer, and telephoned down to the engine room to start all four engines.

"I am outside port limits and do not want to enter Aden," I replied to Port Control.

"It does not matter, you have entered territorial waters and you must clear in." The voice told me.

"I am sorry, I must consult with my owners," I said.

"It does not matter, you must clear in. You have entered territorial waters."

"I will get back to you as soon as I have instructions from my owners," I said.

The anchor was quickly aweigh and with four engines on full power, the "Salvanguard" disappeared over the horizon, with the voice still telling me to come in. I later discovered from a visitor to Aden from Djibouti that the "Salvanguard" was 'posted' for non-payment of port dues and pilot fees.

Djibouti, the capital of the independent state Territoire des Afars and Issas, was hot, dusty and poor unless you were French. It is situated at the bottom end of the Red Sea, instead of turning left for Aden you go straight on.

The Foreign Legion has a large base, the French Navy maintained a considerable presence and the French Army were in residence. Although the Prime Minister was a Djiboutian, and so were the ministers, a lot of the civil servants were French.

There were a couple of trees in the main square Place Menelik otherwise the place was barren and the further inland

I went, the more lunar the landscape became, reminding me of a hot Iceland. The overall colour on the ground is brown and the sky a pitiless blue. In the afternoon the town is dead, everyone takes a siesta. There are more bars – mostly the honky tonk sort – per building than anywhere else I know in the world.

Our agents, Gellatly Hankey, were the Lloyd's agents and the head man was a large, fat man called John, who kept most irregular hours. However, that did not matter because the shipping side was efficiently run and I managed to obtain an open-dated port clearance.

Svitzer, the Danish salvage company, were based in the area for over fifty years at Aden but now they were in Djibouti and Gellatly were their agents as well. There was considerable rivalry and they resented the new Singapore interloper being on salvage station as well. The tugs were of a similar speed and whoever got away first would normally reach the casualty first. There were a couple of runs where the tugs raced neck and neck up the Red Sea but no salvage.

Early in the New Year I received a message to proceed to Assab in Ethiopia and then on up to Massawa. It was not clear if Massawa was in the hands of the government or the Eritrean rebels, hence the need to call at Assab first and clear into Ethiopian waters. I was not feeling very well, suffering from an apparently blocked gut, but I sailed at full speed leaving the Danes guessing!

In Assab I received permission to proceed to the "Global Mariner", aground north of Massawa. The town had fallen and was now in government hands, but the Eritrean rebels still controlled the coast opposite the "Global Mariner". However, they apparently owned no boats or ships and so I should be safe enough. The Ethiopian Navy carried out regular patrols. I should only move along the coast in daylight otherwise the navy might shoot at the tug.

Although it was incredibly hot outside, the accommodation and bridge of the "Salvanguard" were air-conditioned. I was feeling better and sailed early in the morning for the "Global Mariner", proceeding at full speed to arrive there before dark.

The coast line was mountainous, barren and harsh – no place for the weak – and the navigation was tortuous through the reefs.

The "Global Mariner" was abandoned by her Greek crew and had that ghost ship feeling I was becoming used to. I anchored the "Salvanguard" close by and made my survey, while the divers made theirs.

The casualty was hard aground and two of the fuel tanks were open to the sea. She was fully laden with bagged grain – a free gift from the Common Market to the starving Ethiopians. There was not much fuel or fresh water on board. The weather was fine and pelicans were swimming in the vicinity. We were completely on our own here, the barren mountains of Eritrean rebel-held territory visible under the hot, harsh sun.

I laid out the anchors of the casualty with the "Salvanguard" – no easy task with the big tug. We laid ground tackle using the blocks and wires bought from Frank at Interworld and the spare anchor from the ship. The divers were unable to get at the holes in the bottom. We welded on valves and blanks so we could blow air into the tanks and blow out the water.

Fernando and his crew managed to start the generator of the casualty, which provided power to the windlass and winches. When everything was ready the salvage crew on the "Global Mariner" blew the tanks and heaved up tight the chain cable with the windlass and the ground tackle with the winches. I streamed the connected towing gear and towed at full power, throwing the big tug about from side to side to side making her heel with water coming over the tow deck. It was to no avail, the "Global Mariner" would not move. I noticed the pelicans had gone and wondered why.

***

The next day bad weather set in, which kicked up quite a sea. I made another attempt to refloat but, again, there was no sign of movement. Selco now put into operation their planning, and despatched a chartered tug and barge from Jeddah across the Red Sea. The pelicans returned, along with fine weather, when the tug and barge arrived.

I set the salvage crew to work discharging the bagged grain onto the barge. I drove a winch and occasionally, to show willing, worked in the incredibly hot hold. The men were sullen, and when I went on deck early one morning to drive my winch I saw – painted in large letters on the bridge front – 'Slave master. We are not slaves.'

Roger Sario, who was very much a leader, went on leave in Djibouti and the fat second mate was promoted chief officer. He was not going to set the world on fire. In general the crew were normally pretty enthusiastic on a salvage and I asked him what the trouble was about. He told me the crew were tired and wanted an additional bonus for discharging cargo. We had been working pretty hard for four weeks. I asked him why he had not said anything earlier, why wait until not so subtle messages were painted. He just shrugged his shoulders. I had no one to consult with, being the captain, but I was determined to refloat the "Global Mariner", come what may. I agreed to pay a bonus for discharging cargo and reduce the hours worked from 18 to 12. I telexed Singapore.

That night an Ethiopian Navy gunboat came alongside and the commander, a lieutenant, came on board to ask how we were getting on. I did not like the armed guards he posted on the casualty and said so. He told me they would be gone in the morning and returned to his ship.

I was shaken awake by an agitated AB who told me there was trouble on the casualty. I rushed on board and found the Ethiopian Navy had broken open the bonded liquor store. A lot of them were drunk, including the armed guards. I went ballistic with rage, knowing the Greek owners would accuse the salvors of looting. I also carried enough troubles of my own without drunk Ethiopian armed sailors running amok.

I shut the bond locker door, shouted at the sailors to get off my ship, and went back to the tug and onto the gunboat. I pushed past the armed sailor who was pointing his rifle at me and shouted at him to take me to his captain. He was so astonished at this raging, shouting, red-faced Englishman that he complied and took me to the captain's cabin. I barged in and woke the lieutenant, ordering him to take his drunken men off my ship and take his gunboat elsewhere before I complained to his high command. He quickly got dressed and came back with me to the "Global Mariner" and saw the broken padlock on the bond locker, the empty bottles and his drunken sailors roaming around with their rifles. The gunboat was gone within half an hour. There was no more trouble with my crew.

A week later we refloated the "Global Mariner" and reloaded the cargo from the barge. The tug and barge went back to Jeddah and I towed the "Global Mariner" to Massawa. The port officials would not let me bring her in. I was astounded. Ethiopia was supposed to be starving and I had 10,000 tons of free grain on my tow wire.

I anchored the casualty outside the port, left a riding crew on board and entered the next day. The port was empty except for a Russian landing craft and the murdered emperor's yacht. I went alongside the deserted wharf and the few people I could see were not very fat.

The agent, a nervous individual, drove me round in one of the only cars in the place. The shops were empty, and on the other side of the harbour – the north side – it had been flattened in the fighting. The Russian landing craft was loading cases for Aden, ammunition I found out later.

There was one hotel open with one course on the menu – spaghetti – and precious little to go with it except gin, no wine just gin.

I was shown over the old emperor's yacht, and the bath in which he was rumoured to have been suffocated. Edward, my brother, years earlier was in Ethiopia and built a bridge for a leper colony and Emperor Haille Selasse personally gave him a medal.

I was in Massawa for six weeks. Every evening I took the tug out alongside the "Global Mariner", and every morning came back into the harbour. I made friends with the deep-voiced harbour master who said I was welcome to bring in the "Global Mariner" but it was not his decision.

There were meetings after meetings with officials, some of whom were not there the next day for the next round of discussions. Apparently they were eliminated, and there was much shooting at night. Although we were under arrest or at least the tug was, I and my crew were allowed to go ashore and felt quite safe. I used to lunch at the hotel on spaghetti and gin while my crew went ashore in the evenings and liaisons were enjoyed with the local thin girls, there were no fat ones. I discovered the stock of lavatory paper onboard became severely diminished, none being available ashore.

I offered to remove a sunken wreck alongside the wharf, which I did – towing it clear of the wharf and channel. I offered to bring in the "Global Mariner" and put her alongside the wharf myself and I would guarantee Selco pay for any damage I made to the wharf. I offered to take a party out to the Dhalick islands where the Russians had a base. In fact there was a party onboard and I was starting to leave when an armoured car turned up pointing its gun at the bridge ordering me to remain. It was a very frightened party who left the ship. I offered to do anything if they would let me bring in the ship.

Meanwhile, the free grain started to go rotten; and meanwhile, the people starved. It was made quite clear to me that if I tried to make a run for it the Russians would be sent after me to bomb the tug.

Eventually, quite suddenly, I was given a port clearance and told I could go. I picked up the riding crew on the "Global Mariner" and went. We were ordered to return to Singapore. I discovered later that the casualty remained outside the port for eighteen months and the grain completely rotted. A grim example of man's inhumanity to man even your own people.

In Singapore Knobby fitted a crane in place of the derrick for the hold aft, which revolutionised working the tug. Shortly afterwards I was running free at maximum speed up the South China Sea for a ship aground in the dangerous area of unsurveyed reefs. The weather was bad, it was overcast, and I could not get sights. My heart was in my mouth when we entered the unsurveyed area with lookouts posted up the mast and on the monkey island. I told the radio officer to try and get a radio bearing of the casualty to assist me and eventually, after running over shoal water, came up to the "Safina E

Najam".

It was rough, overcast and raining. So rough in fact we could not use the zed boat, so had to feel our way up to the casualty with the tug. Highly dangerous work.

Eventually we got a messenger across, but the casualty crew were dilatory in heaving in the towing gear and the tug went aground. It was the most awful shock to feel the tug hit the bottom and it nearly knocked me off my feet.

I went astern to try and get her off but got the nylon stretcher wrapped round the starboard propeller. Not only was I aground, I was immobilised myself and in need of assistance. The location was miles from anywhere, outside helicopter range, so no one could be rescued. I felt I had let myself and more importantly my crew down but put on a brave face when I went down onto the after deck, the tug pounding and shuddering as she hit the bottom. The brave divers went over into the rough sea and managed to clear the propeller. I went astern and she came off. I made another attempt to connect from a slightly different direction, and this time the crew of the "Safina E Najam" were more successful and we were connected. I slacked out a lot of wire so the tug was in deep water, unfortunately the tow wire lay on top or around coral.

I towed for three days and did everything I could think of with the tug at full power. The weather was foul, with rain and wind, and it was not possible to get any of my salvage crew on board. Waves broke on both sides of the casualty sweeping up to the deck level. A typhoon warning was issued by Hong Kong radio which added additional urgency to the situation. The master told me there was water in the forward holds, and I was beginning to despair of refloating her. Then on the third evening, just as it was getting dark, the "Salvanguard" was towing at full power right on the quarter of the "Safina E Najam" and she started to swing. It was the first movement there had been. I kept turning further to port and the casualty swung more to starboard then stopped. I put the helm hard over to starboard, the tug heeled and moved sideways through the water past right astern of the ship and out onto the other quarter. The casualty started to swing back and then was afloat, rolling in the rough seas. I slowed down and towed her stern first, yawing wildly to the shelter of a reef to the north.

The master informed me over the radio how the water in the forward holds was rising, and I began to think I had refloated her only for the ship to sink on me. The reef, of course, was unlit and it was now the middle of a dark, overcast, wet night and I had to feel my way in to shelter on the radar.

Edgar Selorio, my ex chief officer, arrived with the "Salvanquish" and went straight alongside the "Safgina E Najam" and started to pump. The water started to fall in the holds and I knew we were on the way to success. The next day the divers made an inspection but some of the damage was too great for them to patch.

Edgar loaded his compressor, generator and pumps on board the casualty, together with a salvage crew to run them. Edgar's crew disconnected my towing gear and I put the "Salvanguard" alongside in the 69 position and reconnected to her bow. The "Safina" was 10 feet by the head so, when I started to tow, she yawed out to one side and luckily stayed there. The tow was uneventful, if rough to begin with, and the pumps contained the water. The typhoon passed well to the north of us.

I sent a navigational warning to Singapore radio requesting all ships to keep clear. Off Horsburgh Light, in broad daylight, a ship passed between the tug and the tow. I was very tempted to speed up rather than slow down and take his propeller off with the towline, but I restrained myself and behaved.

I towed the "Safina" into Eastern Anchorage and after she was anchored, left Edgar in charge with the "Salvanquish" alongside.

The tug was bunkered and stored, and I was about to set sail for Labuan when a Norwegian tanker ran aground in Philip Channel.

Hughie Murray was put in charge of the salvage, much to my disgust because I was senior. It was a lightening job and I piloted the small lightening tanker alongside the casualty and then alongside another larger tanker running a shuttle service.

On the third trip at night I botched going alongside the

anchored, partly-loaded, tanker. Alan Bond was on deck and he shouted for me to hold the small tanker alongside while they made us fast. I had gone alongside too far aft and squashed part of my tanker's accommodation under the quarter of the other tanker and nearly squashed the chief engineer, too. Although why the chief engineer was in his bunk when the ship was being manoeuvred I do not know. The next day the "Salvanguard" was connected and I towed the tanker off stern first, narrowly missing a shoal.

There was little damage to the Norwegian ship so it was decided to reload her just outside Western Anchorage and I was the designated pilot.

The night before I was to perform the pilotage I was called out in the middle of the night to a sick AB. I attended and found him curled up in the fetal position. When I tried to straighten him I saw his guts were hanging out. Jesus, I thought, and rushed up onto my bridge where I called Ops and told them to get "Salvital" quick, meanwhile patch me into a doctor. The doctor told me to push in the guts as best I could and tie the wound up with a towel. No one would assist until I got angry and then the second officer agreed to help. There had been a knife fight and no one wanted to be involved. He and I did as the doctor instructed but it was very difficult and we could not push in all the slimy innards so tied it up as best we could. We put him on board the "Salvital" and he was rushed to hospital.

During my pilotage I received a message that the AB was alive, having been on the operating table for four hours, and would recover.

Once the pilotage was successfully completed I took the tug at maximum speed to Labuan Bay. I towed a VLCC back to Singapore from the lay up anchorage in Labuan Bay, the interest being in the size of the tow. Very few ships of this size had been towed before but the "Salvanguard", with her clean free towing gunwale, performed very well and there were no problems.

I returned to Labuan and towed a gas carrier, also to Singapore, for refit after being laid up in the recession.

LLOYDSMAN / SALVISCOUNT

Selco purchased what had been the biggest tug in the world when she was built – the United Towing's "Lloydsman". I flew to Rotterdam with Knobby for a familiarisation trip to Hull, where we were due to take over. She was big, 265 feet long and high out of the water, especially if not well bunkered. Fully bunkered, with over 1,500 tons of fuel, she drew 28 feet – the same draught as a loaded freighter. This was not so much a tug, more a small ship.

She was single screwed, with two engines coupled to a single shaft through a flywheel that weighed 54 tons. The master, an old Pangbournian although I had not known him, warned us that if she went aground she would fall over due to her underwater shape, which was cut away aft. Sure enough the tug went aground, waiting to enter the lock in Hull, and fell over to a 15 degree list.

Captain Gaston greeted us in his loud voice. "I am taking you both out to lunch and don't forget to tell Mr Kahlenberg, whom you moaned to that we never gave you lunch when you brought the "Statesman"." (Now "Salvanguard") Which was true. They never bought us a drink, let alone lunch!

There was no strike so we stayed on the East coast and dry docked her in Middlesbrough at Smith's dock. That was an illuminating insight as to why the UK was falling behind the rest of the world. The UK seemed to be in another century compared to Singapore. The men turned up for work and did nothing until the foreman arrived an hour later and they were hampered because the managers and white collared workers did not arrive for another hour. The men knocked off work for lunch at noon for an hour but with no canteen. The foremen ate in their own canteen. The managers knocked off at 13:00 for gin and tonics and a silver service lunch with wine at 13:30, arriving back in the offices replete at about 14:30. Everyone went home at 16:30. It could not last and Smiths dock closed down shortly after we departed.

I took the now christened "Salviscount" to Southampton to pick up the salvage gear from Frank of Interworld. We bunkered alongside the berth, opposite where the QE2 berthed and most unfortunately there was a spill and a small quantity of fuel went in the water. The law is quite clear – putting oil in the water is a crime, there are no extenuating circumstances. There was detergent on board but not enough. I telephoned the agent and told him to get some more down quick, and instructed the crew to mop up on deck. By the time I had been reported and the police turned up, all was clean and tidy. However, pollution is taken so seriously that a police inspector was sent to lecture me on what a naughty boy I had been! I was the master therefore I was to blame, even though it was the chief engineer's fault, or possibly shoreside for pumping too quickly. The tug was designed to run on diesel oil, but it was prohibitively expensive so Knobby converted her to heavy fuel, which would make her competitive in the towing market. The only problem was the winter was coming on and it was necessary to heat the fuel.

We did sea trials in the Solent with various guests on board, including my mother. We achieved a speed of 18 knots over the measured mile, creating a huge wash much to the annoyance of a couple of people out for a sail.

When all was ready, I took up salvage station off Yarmouth, Isle of Wight, in the Solent in view of Thorns Beach my mother's house. We were anchored there for a long time with no luck. I took the zed boat to Thorns to see my mother, and for the crew to cut a Christmas tree.

I purchased my mother's scow "Molette" and sailed her back to the "Salviscount". My firefly was called "Mole" and painted black, as was "Molette". My mother purchased a newer scow and called her "Moletta".

I, or rather the pilot, took the tug back to Southampton for stores. One evening I received a telephone call from Alan Schofield of Samuel Stewart, the salvage brokers, who told me that we had a contract on a coaster, the "Activity", anchored off Clovelly, North Cornwall.

It was blowing a full gale and when I called for a pilot they told me it was storm force 10 in the channel. The pilot refused to take me out through the Needles Channel, saying it was too dangerous even for my mighty tug.

We went out through Spithead and once I had dropped him off in the pilot boat, I increased to full speed. Once clear of the Isle of Wight it was very rough indeed, blowing south-west force 9 to 10, and the "Salviscount" was shipping seas right over the wheelhouse. It was a very dark, overcast night and I passed outside the race off Portland Bill.

The weather moderated to gale force 8 the next day rounding Land's End, and there was a fair wind up the North Cornish coast – arriving off Clovelly after dark. The lifeboat was standing by the "Activity", which was not much larger than the "Salviscount" but at least she was loaded.

The son of Captain Gaston was my supernumerary chief officer and Roger Sario was chief officer. I anchored ahead of the coaster and dropped back, using the engine as necessary. It was blowing very hard but we made the connection and I towed her to off Cardiff, where a harbour tug picked her up. It was a Selco first, a salvage in European waters, and a nice hit in the eye for the European salvors – especially Smits and Wjsmuller, the kings of the salvage world.

I had a free hand to take up station where I felt like, so went to Milford Haven; but did not like it so took up station off Falmouth. Fox's were the efficient agents for us and all the Eastern Bloc factory fishing ships, both in and outside Falmouth. The UK fishing boats, loaded to the gunwales with mackerel, sold their catch to the factory ships. I made my number with the coastguards.

One wild night the Rumanian factory ship, "Oltet", dragged her anchor and hit the "Salviscount" on the starboard bow. I was not pleased. I had been on the bridge all night using the main engine to maintain position to prevent the tug dragging.

Shortly afterwards I heard a distress message and called for a pilot. "You must be joking." was the reply so I sailed without. It was blowing storm force 10, and I steamed out at full speed to maintain steerage on a wing and a prayer because

I could not see some of the buoys. I somehow felt the "hand of God" was with me. My crew were fantastic despite never having experienced winter weather like it.

Outside it was very rough indeed once we were outside the lee of the land. A tug towing a barge was in difficulties. The barge was adrift and I went for the barge, while Wjsmuller went for the tug.

The next morning I found the barge and asked the coastguards if they could send a helicopter so I could lift a man on board the drifting barge. It was blowing too hard, helicopters were all grounded.

The emergency pick up line was entangled in the dangling, broken towing gear and although I went as close as I dared, the crew were not able to pick it up. The motion of the tug was violent in the heavy seas. I could do nothing until the weather moderated, but it did not moderate before the barge ran aground off Fowey. I anchored off.

The pilot boat came out and the pilot did a con job on me and – as Dennis Rixon later pointed out – I should have known better. The pilot said I required his services because the tug was in port limits, so I accepted. The pilot boat went back into Fowey and came out with empty beer barrels, which we tied onto the tow wire. The barge was aground in such a way that there was no lee side. It was essential to get someone onto the barge or we could not make a connection. Rene, the zed boat driver, said he could do it. The seas were breaking over the barge, but every now and then there would be a lull. He said he could put someone on the barge in the lulls. If he got it wrong then there would be a fatality. It was cold, the end of December and still rough. Behind the barge were rocks. My heart was in my mouth when he took off with Gaston and stood by just outside the breakers. Suddenly he shot in alongside, Gaston scrambled up a hanging line, and as a breaker went curling in, the zed boat shot out – leaping over the wave before it broke. He had done it.

After a lot of effort and help from Eurosalve, a company engaged by Selco, who got men onto the barge from the cliffs above, the tow wire was connected floated down on the beer barrels brought out by the pilot boat. I picked up the anchor and started towing building up to full power when the beer barrels attached to tow wire lifted out of the water. At high water the barge, Intermac 600 and her intact cargo, was successfully refloated and I towed her to Falmouth putting her alongside at Falmouth docks. It was a very good salvage in almost the ultimate of bad weather and my Filipino crew behaved magnificently. I anchored in the harbour.

The next day it snowed and my crew were thrilled, never having seen snow before. My mother turned up for a few days having driven through the snow on a whim! Dennis Rixon arrived to take evidence and was very awkward and irritable, taking ten days to do what should have taken two. His diabetes was not helped by all the wine and beer consumed.

We had been on the UK coast for six months now and my Filipino crew being well educated read the newspapers, unfortunately far too many "Daily Mirrors" and the like with socialistic nonsense reporting. They were thoroughly fed up with the cold and rain. In 90 days we endured 45 gales. I phoned Alan Bond in Singapore and told him I thought we better move the tug to Spain or Portugal before trouble started.

A telex arrived shortly afterwards instructing me to proceed to Toulon in the South of France. Just past Gibraltar, Rene the fantastic boat driver, threatened to kill me and to this day I do not know why. He flew back to Singapore from Toulon.

The engineers were having problems with the Pielstick engines when they were both connected to the shaft. One would be lazy and do no work, while the other one worked overtime – the balancing gear was not functioning properly. Knobby flew down to the South of France and fixed it, while we prepared the drill ship we were contracted to tow to Singapore. I enjoyed a couple of meals ashore in the expensive, but good, restaurants.

I started the tow in fine fettle but then things started to go wrong and, by the time I reached Port Said, not only were the engines not balancing, one engine did not work at all. Sayeed Hassan, our private agent, turned up on board and when I told him what had happened, he said keep quiet or the Canal

Authorities might not let us through or impose additional tugs at vast expense. The master of any ship passing through the canal has to fill in and sign a form that, among other things, states the engines are in good working order. To falsify the information is a serious offence. I did not fancy an Egyptian jail, on the other hand I wanted to get Selco's new super tug to Singapore with her tow. I, therefore, falsified the form, stating that both engines were working satisfactorily. The canal transit, towing the drill ship, was completed without incident but it was a tense transit for me.

Pielstick experts were waiting for us in Djibouti, where we anchored for four days. The drill ship captain was getting fed up with the delay, and I did not help by sailing my black scow "Molette" in the afternoons. I claim it to be the only time ever a Beaulieu scow has ever been sailed in Djibouti.

The air-conditioning on the "Salviscount" packed up as well and the accommodation was incredibly hot. Being designed for air-conditioning, the port holes could not be opened. Tempers began to be on a very short fuse. It was cooler when we were again under way, with the experts remaining on board.

A few days after leaving Djibouti I received a telex instructing me to pick up and tow a fishing boat which had broken down. I decided to wait until I reached the casualty before I informed the drill ship captain.

It was a valuable Japanese fishing boat with a full catch, but she was only a quarter of the size of the "Salviscount." The drill ship master was most cooperative and we quickly connected up the Japanese boat and arrived in Singapore with two tows!

I was glad to be back in Singapore but not very pleased when Ops told me that Major Crafter was coming out on the company yacht with guests to look over Selco's latest acquisition. It was a Sunday, the garbage had not been collected by the port refuse boat, the air-conditioning still did not work, and the tug was not in a condition for an inspection. "Salvalentina" came alongside and the beach-dressed party came on board.

Remarks like, "Oh, doesn't the air-conditioning work?" And, "Isn't it hot in here?" did not endear them to me.

And when Crafter complained about eggshell in the garbage, I said, "Don't you read the telexes any more?"

To which he replied, "Oh, no, I am in the town office. These are bankers who have loaned Selco money, and they wanted to see our latest asset."

I gave him a quick resume of the voyage and he said, "You had better join the party but don't say anything to the bankers."

So I had a day out on the yacht, which was fun – swimming, booze and sun, but no sex!

SALVAGE MASTER

"Salviscount" was the last tug I was permanently in command of and I handed her over to Edgar Selorio, my ex chief officer, and came ashore. I was promoted salvage master and marine-superintendent, and lived in the Orchard Hotel, at the top of fashionable Orchard Road.

Knobby and I accompanied the tug, towing a barge with a huge six-storey high desalination plant as cargo bound for the Middle east. In the Malacca Straits the tug suffered a blackout and the tow overtook the tug, missing a collision by inches. Many grey hairs were added to my already grey head! Edgar was master but he had no more problems successfully delivering his tow. Knobby and I went ashore off Penang and returned to Singapore.

There were considerable changes in the office. Alan Bond was looking after the scrap ship project with Crafter, who had been removed to the town office and was out of the way. Hancox was now running Selco, Mr K ever present in the background. I was supposed to be marine-superintendent but I was not really interested; salvage was my interest.

The "President Eisenhower" ran aground opposite the light at the Southern end of the Malacca Straits on the Malaysian side. I thought I would be the salvage master but Captain Hancox decided to do it, leaving me in the office.

I drove to the casualty's Singapore superintendent's house on a Sunday and we signed the LOF, unfortunately managing to sign in the wrong place. I signed as the owner and the superintendent signed as the salvor.

Hancox was in his seventh heaven with tugs and barges and a crane barge to direct. The "President Eisenhower" ran aground at full speed and her bow was 18 feet into the mud. She was a large container ship and a considerable number were discharged onto a Selco barge before the "Salvanguard," and other assorted Selco tugs, pulled her off undamaged. I was not very pleased to have been left ashore because I missed out on a good salvage bonus.

I saw quite a lot of Mr K and sometimes went out for a drink. Something had changed in Selco – now a highly successful world class salvor. Some of the fun was gone, people were more tense and I think, although he never said anything, he realised Dave Hancox was a better salvor than he was manager. A good manager organises himself so that he does not fall asleep at his desk at midnight and is found there the next morning, salvage operations excepted.

I flew to Japan in my role as marine-superintendent to take over another tug EEK had bought. She required a lot of work, having been laid up for years, and an engineer consultant looked after the engine room.

She was in a small yard on the inland sea near Hiroshima and no one spoke any English, but it was an interesting six weeks. I was glad when it was over and the tug sailed from Japan, smart in her new Selco colours. She was later hit by an Exocet during the Iran-Iraq war and sank with considerable loss of life. On another occasion I took over yet another tug EEK had purchased – the "Salviva".

The "Bright Vega" was a car carrier and she ran aground on the reef at the North end of the Laccadive islands. I flew to Colombo and joined the Selco tug on salvage standby, sailing that evening.

The ship was very heavily aground on coral and had been lifted bodily up onto the reef. It was going to be very difficult to refloat her, four of her fuel tanks were holed and the divers could not get at them to patch. A serious stability problem would occur if any water got on the car deck because the vessel would capsize.

The "Salvanguard", towing an empty barge, was sailing from from the Persian Gulf, and when she arrived the barge was placed alongside the casualty. We ran ground tackle from the car deck and drove the cargo of buses onto the barge via the side ramp. All the remaining bunkers were discharged into the barge and anything movable was loaded onto the barge, including lifeboats and portable tween decks.

The Korean crew were helpful but only the master spoke minimal English, and I do not speak any Korean. The recognised international language of the sea is English. Therefore, the crew who steer the ship and the officers who carry out his instructions are supposed to speak English but this was not the case and communications were very difficult however we managed.

When all was ready – the ground tackle heaved tight, the two tugs connected, the fuel tanks blown with compressed air, I was on the bridge of the "Bright Vega" with my Selco radio – we made a refloating attempt. She did not move. The tide was falling on the tide gauge that we placed on the reef so I ceased the attempt and sent the divers down to have a look. No sign of movement at all. The next high tide was not until that night, so I went off on a picnic with Edgar and some of the salvage crew. We took the zed boat through the lagoon to a small sand spit island, where we found remains of a fisherman's camp.

While we were there an open boat turned up from Kadmat Island, and one of the policemen recognised me from the "Pacifico Everett", in particular the "Salvaliant" towing the "Majma."

That night the "Bright Vega" refloated after towing at full power with both tugs – the whole operation being much more difficult in the dark. The weather was fine so I anchored the "Bright Vega" and drove the mini buses back onto the car carrier and reloaded all the movable equipment. When the barge was empty the "Salvanguard" continued on her voyage to Singapore. The next day the divers patched the holes in the bottom.

It was an interesting feature that the salvage was performed on the Japanese Form rather than Lloyd's Form, which meant a lot of paperwork for me. I listed every piece of equipment used during the operation, made up what it was worth and what we did with it. Selco received a very good award.

The "Sun Aster III" ran aground fully laden north-bound in the Suez Canal. I flew to Cairo and was met by Sayeed Hassan, the owner of Port Said Navigation and Shipping Co.

He was very excited and was sure we could get the contract to salve the ship provided the right people were looked after. Smits were in Egypt trying to obtain the contract as well. The first thing to do was get permission from the Suez Canal Authority, and he knew just the people to go and see.

The next month was spent travelling between Cairo and Port Said, Cairo and Suez, and Cairo and Ismaelia; and on one day we did all three. Finally, I did obtain permission after Alan Bond arrived from Singapore with a brief case full of cash. Once we obtained the permission, the Japanese agreed Lloyd's Open Form. Part of the 'deal' with the Suez Canal Authority was an insurance from Lloyds with an unlimited guarantee for pollution which after negotiation was finally limited to fifty million dollars.

We lightened the "Sun Aster III", discharging part of the cargo into a chartered tanker I manoeuvred alongside. Finally, with the "Salviva" connected, I refloated the tanker.

The termination ceremony was marred by the owners' English lawyer wanting to qualify the letter, to which I would not agree. It was a sign of the change in the salvage world with lawyers interfering on site, which is not to the benefit of anyone – except the lawyers.

I stayed in Egypt, with the "Salviva" in Suez. Together we salved the "Gay Fidelity", which had been on fire and nearly sank under my very feet in the Red Sea while under tow. The after deck was awash when we finally anchored her and put the tug alongside to pump. I was alone on the sinking ship while she was being towed. None of the "Salviva" crew would join me, they thought I was mad and it was a strange sensation, especially at night, wondering how long she was going to remain afloat. I stupidly went into the flooded engine room and slipped damaging my leg and losing the only torch. Shades of the "Flying Enterprise" came to mind but it was not the English Channel so no press coverage. We anchored her outside Suez port limits and managed to obtain termination. I lived in the Red Sea Hotel overlooking the Suez canal.

I salved the "San Juan", which ran aground on the same reef as the "Mare." There were two other wrecks on the reef and she managed to be in between them. It was a real saga just to reach the casualty, chartering a German motor yacht from Hurghada. We were forced to to jettison half the cargo to get her off and take her to Suez with the "Salveritas." The "Salviva" was in the Mediterranean with a tow for Alexandria.

***

I went to London to give evidence and attend an arbitration. It was very interesting to see how the legal system worked again, and emphasised the importance of good the evidence.

SELCO SOLD / LARGEST SHIP IN WORLD

When I returned to Singapore it was all change. Mr Kahlenberg was gone. The dynamo, the driving force, the heart of Selco was gone. He sold out to a Chinese, Peter Tham, whom I never met. Mr K was supposed to have remained as chairman but there was a row and he was pushed out, and with him the soul of Selco.

Peter Tham's henchman, Tam Yen Fei, was the managing director; a Miss Wee was the personal manager; and a runaway Englishman, Roy Croft, was Tam Yen Fei's assistant. A whole new layer of management was in place, with William Crafter as chairman, none of whom knew anything about salvage.

The old one-storey office was abandoned and a new four-storey block built, with the top floor empty – except for the lawyer, Carol Wong. The third floor was furnished with a plush chairman's office – with bathroom, which was never used – and Tam Yen Fei; the second floor housed Alan Bond, Dave Warner, marketing, and the offshore people; the ground floor with Daniel boon, Miss Wee and their assistants. I never saw the senior accountant who worked in the town office.

Elbourne Mitchell, who had been Selco's London lawyers since the beginning, were sacked and Constant and Constant appointed. Their telex answerback was 'two cnts' and I leave it to your imagination to insert the letter near the end of the alphabet which is what I thought of them. Old Selco was finished, the fun and the enthusiasm gone, but salvage was still a fascinating game.

I was glad to fly to the Gulf where I joined the "Salvalour" for a salvage in Oman which was successful. I was ashore in Fujairah when I received a message to rejoin the tug which was at sea and we proceeded a full speed to Shah Allum shoal just inside Iranian waters. The "Wind Enterprise" was aground. She was loaded with 357,000 tons of crude oil and was the biggest loaded ship in the world ever to have run aground. When I arrived on site she looked huge, gigantic, but that was above the water and like an iceberg, more of her was under the water. Her draught was more than sixty feet. She was a lot bigger than the "Showa Maru" and I did not have the facilities and convenience of a home base close at hand. The war between Iran and Iraq had started but it was a land war and was not yet affecting the waters of the Persian Gulf. I took a deep breath and put on my most confident smile when I went up to the captain's cabin – a long climb from the boat.

The Norwegian captain was very subdued, which was not too surprising in the circumstances, and we signed Lloyd's Form. I took on an awesome responsibility, if I screwed up a la "Tojo Maru" I would bankrupt the company and maybe kill a few people as well. A ship loaded with volatile crude oil – especially one as big as this – was not a safe thing. If one of the tanks became holed and leaked oil around the ship I would have a potential huge bomb on my hands. Add to that we were off the coast and in the territorial waters of a Moslem country at war with another Moslem country. It was no wonder I felt tense.

Selco chartered a 100,000 ton lightening tanker, flew special pneumatic fenders up from Singapore, and a salvage team with Captain Ventura in charge of it. Captain Carter was hired from London as safety expert. They chartered Grey Mackenzie tugs to transport them out to me and provide assisting tugs to berth the lightening tanker. The Selco tugs "Salvalour" and "Salveritas" were connected astern and used as ground tackle at first. When all was ready, the tanker was berthed. I gave each tug a radio code, which we used so as to mislead the Iranians. To keep the "Wind Enterprise" firmly aground during the discharge we ballasted her down.

Once enough cargo was discharged I unberthed the lightening tanker, the tugs picked up their anchors and the ballast was pumped out. I watched the tide gauge we put on the reef and, just before high water, I instructed the tugs to commence towing.

The tugs looked small from the bridge of the huge tanker as

she started very slowly to move. I put the main engines astern and the "Wind Enterprise" slid off the reef into deep water. There was no pollution, which indicated that all the tanks were still intact. I was in a hurry to get out of Iranian waters before a gunboat turned up and caused trouble.

The chief engineer reported that the main engine was undamaged so, once the tugs were disconnected, I piloted the refloated ship to Dubai at slow speed, leaving the fenders alongside. I reberthed the lightening tanker and the cargo was reloaded. When the lightening tanker was clear, and all the equipment reloaded onto the tugs, termination was signed and I heaved a huge sigh of relief. We had been successful – it was a world record.

NAME AT LLOYDS

While rushing about the Egyptian desert in motor cars during the "Sun Aster III" salvage, I had lots of time to contemplate and I thought it would be a good idea if I could join Lloyds, the insurance market, as a Name. It would give me a fantastic entry to the insurance world, who ultimately, were the paymasters of salvors. The previous year, on one of my trips to London, Molly Julian introduced me to the then chairman of Lloyds Peter Green, later Sir Peter, and we enjoyed a dinner together. If I had enough money he thought it was a good idea. He also explained to me the checks and balances in the system to keep salvors and underwriters happy at the same time. Salvors were complaining the salvage awards were not large enough to keep them in business. He said the pendulum was swinging and no doubt the awards would go up and the overall median figure achieved.

On one of my trips to Djibouti I stayed in the Paris Athénée Hotel, very expensive but very good. I wrote on the hotel notepaper to Edward's father-in-law, who was a Lloyd's Name and asked if I could join.

Robert Gaynor, Ginnah Borthwick's husband, agreed to second me and I was introduced to Anne Davison from Willis Faber, who would look after me. I arranged with my local Barclay's Bank manager to put up a bank guarantee for £100,000 to Lloyds. Anne took me to my rota committee meeting, where it was quite categorically explained to me that I was liable individually for my losses, down to my last brass farthing.

It was most impressive sitting behind the large table in that grand room with the committee on the other side. The spokesman meant what he said. I stated that I understood and that was that. I never believed that I would sustain such losses, that bankruptcy would become an option, little did I know what fate had in store for me. I was on the way up, on a roller coaster and I wanted to stay with it for the ride – the future looked bright and rosy. The only slight puff of a cloud in the distant horizon was my friend Ray Clarke from Elbourne Mitchell who said, with that quizzical look in his eye, "I hope you know what you are doing."

MANAGING SELCO

I was in Djibouti when I received a telephone call from Alan Bond.

"Get yourself back to Singapore immediately," he instructed.

"What for?" I asked.

"Just do as you are told for once," he commanded. Bond might be a man of few words, but he was not usually quite so blunt.

I caught the next plane to Paris, again stayed in the Paris Athénée, and then on to Singapore, arriving tired in the office. I did not remain tired for long.

"I am sick. I have cancer and been given three months to live. I am taking some time off and you are in charge." And with that he left the office and did not return.

I was dumbfounded. It was so utterly unexpected and with the changes, I thought a Chinese would be put in charge of the salvage and tugs. I sat there in his chair and thought. What am I going to do? How am I going to do the job? I then thought, well, if I owned the company what would I do? And that is what I did. I pretended in my mind to own Selco and operated accordingly.

Mr K was still in Singapore, although he suggested we did not meet in public in case it upset the 'new people'. So I met him at his flat or Alan's house. I saw Alan at his home and made a pact with him. I would do my best to run Selco and if he recovered I would relinquish his chair back to him. Alan went off to the Cameron Highlands, and later to the Bristol Centre in England for the terminally ill. I did not expect to see him again.

It was an incredibly tense and dramatic time for me. The company was very busy and at one time, I was masterminding eight salvage operations all on the go at the same time. I was spanning the world time zones from New York to Tokyo and was telephoned at any hour. The trick on wakening to the telephone call in the middle of my night was to recognise the voice so I could talk about the caller's ship. An owner is mightily offended if you talk about someone else's ship to him. For six weeks I never had more than a couple of hours sleep at a time.

I was much resented by the Chinese; and P P Wee, a salvage master, and Miss Wee, the personnel manager, actively tried to undermine me. They were both devious and twisted and P P was always so smiling and polite, while shoving in the knife. Miss Wee was so poisonous that I just ignored her.

I thought at first that Tham Yen Fei was intelligent and that his slow speech was a sign of him thinking. He was a very big man for a Chinese but always looked half asleep, and I realised in the end that he was out of his depth as far as salvage was concerned so I ignored him too. Luckily he did not try and interfere. And I froze out Roy Croft, although was quite happy to have a beer with him.

The one bright star was Captain Chua. He had cancer but mostly recovered, and was alive on one lung. He gave me his unstinting support and worked as hard as I did. We worked well together and trusted each other.

My mother came out for Christmas and stayed in the Tanglin Club – the main social club in Singapore – courtesy of Chris Herbert. She met Bill Crafter and declared him a phoney. She was taken around by various wives, going to Sentosa on the cable car, and visiting all the sights.

I was living in the Orchard Hotel at the top of Orchard Road, opposite the Ming Court Hotel where we had an enjoyable Christmas and New Year celebration. I was a Name at Lloyds at the comparatively early age of 40 all by my own efforts, I was not unknown in the salvage world, and I was running Selco Salvage, with its large fleet of tugs and barges. I had something to celebrate.

A Greek ship on the way to China suffered an engine breakdown off the North coast of Sumatra. The "Salveritas", with Crowther in command, reached the drifting ship first and signed a Lloyd's Form with the master. While connecting, Crowther reported a Smits arrived on the scene and the master said they had a Lloyd's Form agreed in Piraeus. I was in Ops and telexed back instructing Crowther to tell the Smit tug politely to push off, the master's signature was better than anyone else's (shades of the "Unique Mariner"). Crowther telexed back that they were under way but the Smit tug was still alongside.

'Cut his lines,' I telexed back.

Shortly afterwards an irate Roy Martin, the Smit manager in Singapore, telephoned and asked me what I thought I was doing, someone would get killed. I asked him icily what he thought he was doing muscling in on my salvage. Therein ensued an argument on the relative merits of the signature on a Lloyd's Form. Did a Lloyd's Form reputedly agreed but not signed in Piraeus before the signing of the Lloyd's Form by the master take precedent? I said I was quite happy to see him in court, meanwhile tell his tug to keep clear of the "Dumbaia" or I would take out an injunction against Smits. He rang off and Crowther had no more trouble from Smits. Selco and Smits were the main salvors in Singapore and there was no love lost between them; the rivalry and competition was intense.

The next day Roy Martin asked me out to lunch and I agreed, feeling a bit like the Biblical Daniel entering the lions' den. We had a very pleasant lunch with good wine. We agreed line cutting was not a good idea and the Lloyds Arbitrators might take a dim view. In future we should talk and prevent a "Dumbaia" incident again. Smits would take no action over their alleged Lloyd's Form if I agreed. Well, I was pretty certain Selco would win in court but I saw no harm in preventing a "Dumbaia" incident again, it was not edifying to be in the line cutting business. The "Dumbaia" was towed to China on the Lloyd's Form and grossed a million dollars for Selco.

Alan Bond – against all the odds – recovered and returned, but he did not wholly take back his chair. He left me to run things and moved upstairs, but not for long.

The Iran-Iraq war took on a new and ugly turn and moved out onto the clean waters of the Persian Gulf. The Iraqis were using French made and sold Exocet missiles against shipping in the river to Bushire, but they soon moved further afield.

Alan, his wife and I were being entertained by the Townleys, Keith Townley was the salvage association principal surveyor in Singapore. We were eating New Zealand oysters and drinking a cold, white dry wine. The telephone went and a little later Keith said it was Alan Schofield for me or Alan.

"You take it, Ian," said Alan, and so the die was cast. It was Alan Schofield the salvage broker.

"There is a tanker on fire just south of Kharg abandoned. Smits say it's not salvable. Silver Line are offering a Lloyd's Form."

Kharg Island was the main loading port for the export of Iranian oil and vital to their war effort. My brain started working overtime. The ship was in the war zone, Smits say they can't do it, it must be worth a look.

"Agree Lloyd's Form," I said.

"What was all that about?" asked Alan.

"I've agreed Lloyd's Form on a burning tanker south of Kharg," I said, grinning.

"You've agreed it, you can do it. On your bike or, rather, plane," laughed Alan, wiping the grin off my face.

IRAN IRAQ WAR

I saw the pall of smoke almost forty miles away. The salvage association surveyor and I were passengers on an old, not very fast, Grey Mackenzie boat Selco chartered – the "Grey Atlas". The Pakistani master was not very keen to go into the war zone, but a bonus soon put that right.

The pall got thicker as we steamed closer, the barren mountains of Iran now visible. The land war was raging to the north but the sea war was just starting and I was tense. I wondered if I was on one of the syndicates at Lloyds which insured the burning tanker.

The "Al Ahood" – green bows up in the air, stern under water – was blazing fiercely, the accommodation a conflagration, the flames leaping into the air engulfing the whole aft end of the ship. My heart sank as we sailed closer and stopped a short distance off – the very water around the stern of the ship seemed to be on fire. However, after a time, I realised the fire was not getting any worse and the whole of the fore part of the ship was intact. If we could put the fire out, maybe we could salve the ship. For some reason she was not drifting.

'It is possible. Send salvage crew.' I signalled Alan Bond, now fully back in his chair albeit upstairs. I connected the "Grey Atlas" to the bow of the "Al Ahood" as soon as possible to keep the bow up into the wind and keep the flames from spreading forward.

I agreed with Captain Betts, an ex United Towing master, before leaving Singapore that if the ship was salvable he would lead the salvage team. In the event, Captain Ventura arrived with his team - Juanito was magnificent, he led his team from the front. The man in the white boiler suit in the photograph standing in front of the burning accommodation seen all round the world and on the floor at Lloyds is him. As the chartered tugs arrived, so I put them alongside to fight the flames with their fire monitors.

I boarded the "Al Ahood" prior to Juanito's arrival for a look around. While looking in the dark forecastle I had this uneasy feeling that somebody was looking at me. The noise of the burning crude was clearly audible. I knew that two crew members were missing and it was very eerie. Suddenly a furry thing touched my leg. I leapt into the air in fear, my heart pounding. Shining my torch down – it was the ship's cat.

The fire continued to rage, fed by crude oil leaking through into the engine room and burning on top of the water. The noise was continuous. The accommodation was a huge funnel, fanning and ventilating the flames which leapt high above the burning tanker, at night illuminating the whole area. I realised that water alone would not put it out. There was a lot of water power with all the tugs we chartered, but almost no foam. Smits owned the only foam available in the Gulf and they said the ship was unsalvable. The only specialised fire and foam tug in the Gulf was owned by Smits. After considerable deliberation I agreed to sub contract Smits as co-salvors on our Lloyds Form. Selco chartered a jumbo jet to fly out more foam from Europe because there was not enough in the Gulf even with Smits supply. Two supply boats bought out the 20 tons of foam, which we loaded onto the "Al Ahood." After ten days all was ready for the extinguishing attempt. The Smit firefighting expert took charge of the attempt to put out the fire. I put one tug on either side of the towing tug and kept the burning ship bow into the wind. Aad positioned the Smit tug and his team with hoses – the Selco salvage men as back up – and early one morning the attempt was made. Tons of foam were poured onto the accommodation from the tugs' fire monitors and the firefighting team went into it with hoses. Almost all of the foam was used and finally the fire was out. It was incredibly silent after the days of the roaring furnace. Everyone was very conscious that we were in a war zone and if the ship had been attacked once, why not again? Any untoward noise had me and many others jumping.

The fire was out so now I wanted to tow the tanker out of the war zone as quickly as possible. Why she was apparently held by the stern I still did not know, but there was no time to find out if we could move her. I coordinated the eight tugs for towing and the "Al Ahood" started to move. It required constant attention and instructions to maintain any sort of course, but slow progress was made.

I was very tired, not having any sleep for six days and nights, and I asked Hans who was in overall charge of the Smits team and tugs, to take over for a while. Two hours later I was awoken by Juanito for some emergency, so gave up on the idea of sleep. I am still amazed that I was instantly awake and alert, danger does funny things to one.

I was expecting the "Salvanguard" to arrive from Djibouti but she was late. I wanted a big, powerful tug ahead to keep control. We slowly inched our way south and finally heaved a collective sigh of relief when we were out of the war zone.

Shortly afterwards the "Salvanguard" arrived and connected up. The "Al Ahood" started to make better speed – just over two knots – and we finally made the position I decided on outside Bahrain for the ship to ship transfer.

After Juanito let go the "Al Ahood" anchor, I sent the divers down to look at the stern of the casualty which was still under water. It turned out she was fitted with a stern anchor and the force of the missile explosion had blown it off, letting all the chain out, so the ship was effectively anchored by the stern. No wonder she was so difficult to tow. The divers cut the chain and the "Al Ahood" swung round and lay to her bow anchor.

I talked to Martin Eve, whom I had not met before. He was a real live wire, full of enthusiasm, who talked so fast that the words sometimes fell over themselves so he appeared to be stuttering. He was thin and fit.

The previous master of the "Salvanguard" who bought her into into the gulf funked coming into the war zone. Some of the crew were changed as well, led by the bespectacled radio officer who was a nasty piece of work. The Europeans had not set a very good example to the Filipinos and my admiration for Captain Ventura increased even more.

Now that the "Salvanguard" was on site with her radio

officer I was in direct communication with Singapore via telex over radio. I dismissed some of the smaller tugs and made preparations for discharging the "Al Ahood." She was a wreck, the engine under water, the accommodation burnt out and tilted to one side where it had melted. Selco flew up the hydraulically-driven pumps for over the top pumping and pneumatic fenders. Chris Herbert must have been in his seventh heaven.

I let Martin and Juanito get on with the preparations while I dealt with the surveyors and all the shore people who turn up after a major salvage. Even the Press turned up and I was interviewed on the deck of the "Al Ahood," with the bent accommodation as a backdrop. The interview appeared on ITV straight after the visit of President Reagan.

The cat joined the "Salvanguard", becoming fat and sleek.

The "Al Ahood" was loaded with 140,000 tons of crude oil from Kharg Island and about ten thousand was lost in the fire. A Troodos tanker was chartered to carry the entire cargo to destination, but we could not put her alongside until the stern had been lifted. So a second small tanker was chartered and we ran a shuttle service. Martin did the piloting and pre-loading inspections with the London consultants; Juanito ran the salvage crew and pumps; Smits ran their pumps and crew. I was in overall charge and planning. At one stage there were 11 tugs, two tankers and the casualty under my control – 150 people. All the key people carried radios so we had good communications, even with Smits.

The weather turned sour and it blew very hard at times. There were so many shore people wanting to come on board that I chartered a separate tug for them and gave them fixed times to come on board so as not to interfere with the salvage.

The shuttle service ran well and slowly the stern rose out of the water, revealing the huge hole which the exploding missile made. Eventually we put the Troodos tanker alongside and completed the discharge. She took the cargo on to destination.

The pumps and salvage equipment were packed up and the wreck was left with the "Salvanguard" standing by. I then towed and anchored the "Al Ahood" off Dubai. It was eerie when I went onboard her, a burnt out wreck to realise the sunken "Dara" the burnt out passenger ship of my youth was near by. Finally Selco brought the wreck and she was towed to Taiwan for scrap.

In Bahrain I gave my evidence to the Constant and Constant lawyer, while remaining on salvage standby with the tug. Captain Crowther, a Selco master, was our representative in Bahrain and he was due to take over the "Salvanguard" from me. He was so negative and afraid that I phoned Bond and said he should not command the "Salvanguard". That same evening I sailed the tug back to the war zone where Smits had a contract on the "Tiburon" – a loaded tanker bigger than the "Al Ahood" hit by an Iraqi Exocet.

The fire was put out and I towed the "Tiburon" to the "Al Ahood" 's discharge location. Almost as soon as the anchor was down I was off again with Gert Koffeman and his team for the "Chemical Venture". ITC arrived at the same time so they were contracted as well and I towed the "Chemical Venture" to Bahrain after the fire was put out.

If there was an emergency when a tug is at sea they always seem to be able to get away. If the tug is in port there is always some good reason why she cannot sail. The obvious answer was to keep the tug at sea and so I took the "Salvanguard" to sea and we anchored on salvage standby, being supplied by Grey Mackenzie tugs as necessary.

The "Dashaki" was the last field salvage I performed. She was abandoned and adrift after an alleged attack and her engine room was flooded. I nearly got the tug run over when going alongside, having misjudged the speed the ship was drifting. I towed her to Dubai and pumped her out while machinery preservation was performed.

I handed over the tug to a new Selco Chinese master and flew back to Singapore. I took up residence in Bond's old office on the second floor, while he occupied the corner office on the third floor. Martin Eve was salvage master in the Gulf.

BANKRUPTCY

I went back to my old mould and ran Selco Salvage with Captain Chua under Bond's overall supervision, which meant I saw even less of Tham Yen Fei, but something was beginning to go wrong. Selco was making huge sums from the Gulf War yet money was apparently tight. One of my pay cheques bounced, which was explained away as a bank mistake. No one had seen Peter Tham who, apparently, was in overall charge yet he held no executive position in the company.

The sea war raged on and Selco performed many salvage operations which I ran from Singapore, travelling to London for arbitrations and preparing for the "Al Ahood" arbitration. Tham Yen Fei took unannounced days off from the office, as did Miss Wee. There was an air of uneasiness.

The "Al Ahood" award was the biggest salvage award ever at that time. Money was pouring through the door yet the company was not paying its bills.

One day the receivers were in the office, the company was in deep trouble and made bankrupt. The Singapore Stock Exchange was shut for three days, as was the Kuala Lumpur Exchange in Malaysia. It was just not conceivable that the salvage company could be losing money. In fact it was the holding company Pan Electric which were bankrupt but it owned Selco Salvage. It turned out that Peter Tham and Tan Koon Swan, the secretary to Dr Mahathir's ruling party in Malaysia, were engaged in some shady deal which had gone wrong. Both eventually ended up in jail.

I continued on as usual and went to Spain to conclude a deal with Peter Bruce concerning the "Ceyan" and "Vatan" which were hit by exocets and we had salved and were sold for scrap. Both ships were larger than the "Wind Enterprise" some 400,000 tons deadweight. I got him to pay me US$15,000 expenses I had paid with my own money and was not certain the receivers were going to reimburse me. I was right. They did not and I would have been out of pocket.

I tried to keep the show going but the receivers' job was to collect and realise assets, not run a company.

Nikki Tan was charming and polite to me, but I was useful. Personnel were being laid off and the company was running down. Smits wanted to buy Selco and there were other interested parties.

Crafter, the chairman, disappeared. If he knew what was going on he should have stopped it. If he did not know what was going on he should have, he was the chairman and in that, twice damned. He had failed dismally.

I rang Harold Rapp, who used to live in the Log House near Thorns Beach and now owned Dukes Hotel in St James Square. He was interested in joining a syndicate to buy Selco and would find more participants. Mr K, who was in Singapore, agreed to join. Harold rang to tell me he had found interested parties and would I fly to the States to give a presentation. I asked the receivers for permission to go at my own expense, but word came back from the Prime Minister's office that if I left Singapore I would not be allowed back in and Selco ownership would not be allowed to leave Singapore in any event. So that was the end of that idea.

Christoph Bettermann, a German who ran an oil support company in Dubai with boats and an accommodation rig, was interested in buying the tugs and barges. He interviewed me in my office and asked me for a drink in the evening at the Sheraton Park Hotel, where he was staying.

After dinner he offered me a job in Dubai to start a salvage division for him. I was interested because it was quite clear that the Singapore government were going to take over and I did not want to work for the Chinese. I told Bond and he tried to put me off, warning me that he did not trust Bettermann and, anyway, he wanted me to remain with him.

Ray Clarke did a recce of IMS in Dubai and it was favourable. Bettermann sent me a club class return ticket to Dubai and I went up over a weekend and agreed to join IMS as soon as possible. The receivers held me to one month's notice and then did not pay me! I discovered that my pension contributions were never paid into the pension funds, there was no pension and we were not going to get our salvage bonuses, a huge financial loss to me and of course all the other Selco employees.

I flew to Dubai and started a new phase of my life.

DUBAI

It was a charming, affable Christoph Bettermann who was host for the weekend I spent in Dubai. He was a tallish man with a smooth-skinned face and very intelligent. I stayed in the Chicago Beach Hotel, which was close to the villa that he lived in with his wife.

I was introduced to Captain Baudoy, who was marine-superintendent, and his wife who lived in the villa next door; and Herr Schneiders, the German accountant, who lived in the third villa of the complex. We had an enjoyable day by the private swimming poor and dinner at the Sheraton. I was promised a nice apartment, a car and a contract to be negotiated. Everything looked very rosy.

Dubai is very different from Singapore. Singapore is green, lush and sometimes wet; Dubai is dry and brown, the sand is everywhere although flowers are grown between the dual carriageways. A few minutes' drive from Dubai you hit the desert, albeit on a dual carriageway. In Singapore, once clear of the apartments, it was jungle. Dubai, although cosmopolitan, was very Arab; Singapore was westernised Asian. In Dubai the day of rest and worship in the mosque was Friday; in Singapore Saturday and Sunday were free. It was a lot hotter in the summer and colder in the winter than Singapore. Dubai was a Sheikdom, ruled by one man; Singapore was a democratic Republic and it showed in the general atmosphere. I always felt an alien, my sponsor was responsible for my behaviour in Dubai. I had no 'rights' of my own. The expatriate community stuck closer together.

When I arrived in Dubai to start work my heart sank at the airport. It was in the cool of the early morning, the best time of day. Instead of one of the cars I was met by a driver with the office runabout. I was taken to my 'nice' flat and my heart sank further to my shoes. I had made the most almighty mistake, the German had tricked me. Bond had been right. The flat had no servants' quarters, was small, the view looked over a low rent block, and was practically unfurnished. I sat down to think on the only obviously second-hand armchair.

I did not want to work for the Chinese, in fact I would not work for them. I found their money grubbing, tight fisted, rules and regulations, car and driver mentality was not compatible with a salvage company. The fun had all gone.

I had two options. Make a go of it in Dubai and put up with the German. I would make a reasonable amount of money to make up for what I lost in Selco – pay, salvage bonuses, including "Al Ahood", and pension. Or call it quits and go home to England. I was a Name at Lloyds and would find something to do. The second option was not much of a challenge. The first was a challenge, and if I could control the German I could make IMS a world salvor. The tools were there, it was just a matter of using them in the right way. Bettermann agreed that Elbourne Mitchell would be our London lawyers. I had the right contacts in London and I was sure I would succeed. I decided to stay in Dubai and give it a go.

***

No office was ready for me. I made another mistake. The IMS complex was on the starboard side of the creek going in. It consisted of a wharf for the boats, a fabrication yard for the offshore industry, a repair facility for the fleet and two office blocks. The block facing the road was one-storey and built of concrete. The Sahibs of IMS worked there: Bettermann; Schneiders; Suleiman, a Pakastani; and the accountants. Across a courtyard with a concrete floor was a ramshackle wooden building, with a rickety ladder leading onto the second floor. Here was the heart of the IMS fleet: Omar, the business manager, a Palestinian; Alain Baoudy marine superintendent, an Englishman; Chris Loat marketing a retired Royal Navy commander; two secretaries, Dominic an Indian who worked with me and a Sri Lankan; and, most important of all, the Operations room manned by Indians. There was room for an office here and I decided – provided a window was put in and I could see the creek – I wanted to be there with quick access to Ops. In the back of my mind it was far enough away from Bettermann so he could not 'sit' on me. We agreed that I have a free hand to run the salvage, and I intended that was the way it was going to be. Bettermann wanted me to be in the concrete block near him and his secretary, an English girl, Judith. I won. I complained about the flat and he said Judith lived in the block and if it was good enough for her it was good enough for me. I intended only to sleep there so let it go for the moment.

Wjsmuller, the number two Dutch salvage company, were using IMS as their base, but when I arrived on the scene they moved out.

I started with an empty table and a telephone. The first thing to do was to let everyone know where I was, which I did – the salvage brokers being the most important. The next thing was to subscribe to Lloyd's Intelligence and Lloyd's List. I knew people who worked for both which helped.

I set about learning 'my' fleet and its personnel, what equipment was available, and enlisting the support of George, the German engineer-superintendent, and Gordon, the repair man – an Englishman. The Operations room had to be expanded with radios, another telex and more personnel. I started to find out more about Bettermann.

Nothing very much happened at first, there was a lull in the sea war. My very first salvage was a disaster financially. I chartered a tug with an IMS master as salvage master to go to Salalah in Oman and tow in an Eastern bloc ship but unfortunately they repaired the engine and steamed in themselves.

Bettermann was very angry but I became used to his anger and ignored him.

"If you don't like it don't be involved in salvage," I told him.

It was imperative to have a large dedicated salvage tug out on station and a good salvage master. None of the IMS men had any salvage experience so I recruited Martin Eve, who had gone back to England and started a pizza business which was driving him into his grave with boredom.

When I started to spend money Bettermann became difficult.

Bettermann appeared to have a free hand. I say 'appeared' because it later turned out that it was not quite so free as he made out. It was a pity that he did not come clean and tell me what the restrictions were at the beginning because I thought I was dealing with the man who made the decisions. I later discovered that he had to obtain Mohd al Fayed's permission for expenditures over US$25,000 which – in the salvage world – is peanuts if you need to charter a ship or jumbo jet at short notice, or agree a major commission, or even pay the lawyers' fees. Mohd. whom I never met owned IMS. I therefore fought a permanent running battle with the German and acted as though I owned the business and argued later.

It was a real shame that there was no mutual trust because if he had acted differently the final outcome would have been very different. It seemed to me he possessed some vision but not on a world scale and allowed himself to become bogged down in the minutiae of life, instead of holding onto the vision and pushing through to the end goal.

Meanwhile, back in the shop, I had to decide how to beat the competition. Selco – becoming Singapore government's Semco – was almost out of it for the time being. One of their tugs was under arrest in Dubai, and I am ashamed to say I did not go to see them. Arturo Brioso was the master, my chief officer on the "Salviking."

Wjsmuller positioned one tug in the gulf and teamed up with Niko at Al Jadaf, a diving outfit with supply boats. Smits operated a base in Bahrain and later in Sharjah, where IMS also owned a base – the next Emirate east from Dubai and an hour's drive across the desert from the creek. Now that Selco had collapsed I doubted Smits would wish to have much to do with Semco if they came into the gulf – once bitten by the Chinese twice shy.

The IMS base was the key, strategically situated at Dubai. I sent the unemployed tugs, out on salvage standby in the Persian Gulf, to designated stations with code names. I persuaded Bettermann to buy two portable firefighting units for use on the tugs without fire monitors, and a big load of foam. He turned down a fantastic deal with Frank of

Interworld who wanted to base a big load of foam with IMS, in effect giving us foam on sale or return.

Mr K was keen to sell his tug. He bought an old Bugsier salvage tug – the "Pacific" of Amoco Cadiz fame – renamed her "Intergulf", employed Dick Jolly as master and McFarlane as chief engineer, and she roamed the world looking for salvage. She was still very fast and could outrun any tug in the Gulf. I persuaded Bettermann to buy her and Dick Jolly brought her up from Singapore and into the creek.

I was hoping to employ all the crew because they were all keen salvage men and most of them ex Selco. Bettermann came into his own as a mean businessman and reduced all their pay. Those who would not agree were fired and sent home to Manila. Not surprisingly, Dick and McFarlane went home as well. It left a particularly sour taste in my mouth because agreements were not honoured and it was not a good basis to start a salvage operation.

I recruited Dave Stirling, ex Selco, who became her highly successful permanent master, he was a natural seaman and handled her beautifully.

With the "Intergulf" on salvage station as the main salvage tug – equipped with satellite, phone and telex – IMS were beginning to look a bit more professional. I thought Bettermann would have apoplexy when the invoices arrived for the equipment.

"If you don't like it don't be involved in salvage. We are taking on the world's top salvors and it won't be cheap to beat the competition," I told him.

Then it started. I was awakened in the middle of the night. The "Medusa" was hit in the North Persian Gulf and on fire. I despatched the "Intergulf" and shortly afterwards was phoned by Mr K who told me that the owners' agent was offering a Lloyd's Form provided I agreed an address commission and told me the amount. My competition were Smits and Wjsmuller. No one had heard of IMS, although they had heard of me. I was contacted by Samuel Stewart the salvage brokers, who agreed to work with me, presumably until Semco was up and running. Bond, of course, would have nothing to do with me, he considered I had betrayed him. So if Samuel Stewart worked with me, Bond might not work with them.

I was phoned by the owners' agent, I agreed the commission and IMS was awarded the Lloyd's Form. I told Ops to telex Smits and Wjsmuller that we had been awarded the LOF.

I informed Bettermann the next morning of our success and the commission. He became very angry so I told him that either I ran the salvage my way, which would be successful, or he could do it and I would go home. He saw that I meant what I said and backed down. He did not have the expertise himself and he knew it. He had hired one of the few people in the world who could make it work, and if IMS was to be a salvor he needed me. I won but at considerable cost. He left me alone and I experienced no more trouble, but it was an uneasy truce. As a matter of courtesy I kept him informed but that was all.

The "Medusa", although in ballast, was a VLCC, but still valuable if not too badly damaged. The "Intergulf" was successful and the LOF was terminated.

I was in touch with Ray Clarke on the question of security; how much money should be put up by the owner from which IMS, as salvors, could be remunerated? It was no good salving a ship if we were not going to be paid, and, by putting up a guarantee, the owner maintained control of his ship. If an owner did not put up a guarantee – or pay the salvors – then I was entitled to arrest the ship. We agreed a figure and Ray dealt with the owners' solicitors and a guarantee was arranged and put up at Lloyds. Bettermann began to realise IMS was now in the big league when he saw the size of the guarantee that was put up. I, or rather IMS were on the way.

Ray came out to take the evidence and prepare our case for arbitration. The system works as follows. I had obtained a Lloyd's Open Form 'No Cure No Pay' contract to salve the "Medusa" and bring her to a safe place. This had been done. IMS were successful, having 'cured' the patient "Medusa", and now wanted to be paid. Salvors are really doctors of the sea; if you are sick you call the doctor and he cures you. However, when he sends in his bill you tell him, "Jesus, doctor, I was not that ill!" So with a ship owner, his ship is in trouble and he calls for a salvor and when the salvor asks for payment, he says, "Christ, it was not that bad, we could have done it without you." If the two sides cannot agree they call in the Arbitrator appointed by Lloyds.

The contract stipulates the way security should be put up, which had been done, and the appointment of a Lloyd's Arbitrator. You cannot go to the arbitrator and say, "Mr Arbitrator, I have done a fantastic salvage job with lots of dangers and the ship is nice and valuable and we have been very skilful, please pay me lots of money."

The Arbitrator wants to know the hows and whys, he needs the evidence of what you have done – hence the need for Ray to take statements from the participants. We know the owners' solicitors are going to downgrade the salvage, and their participants are going to say, 'Well, we really did not need them but they did turn up with a tug, only give them a small amount of money.' So the skill of the salvor's lawyer is to show the salvage in the best light, and show the Arbitrator – through the evidence – that the operation was professionally carried out and that the salvors are committed to salvage with salvage tugs, equipment and personnel.

I had known Ray for many years and trusted his sage advice. He was no stuffy lawyer living in an ivory tower giving ambiguous advice, he was down-to-earth, living in the real world with a knowledge of the possible. He could argue the minutiae of the law with the best of them and did so when necessary.

Mike Harrison of Clyde and Co solicitors, who acted for a lot of cargo interests, called on Mr Bettermann to persuade him to use Clydes as IMS solicitors. Clydes acted for Mohd Al Fayed, so used that as a lever. However, one of my criteria for working with IMS was that Elbourne Mitchell would be our London solicitors. I was not about to change my mind and switch to a legal 'factory'. I met Mike when I worked with Elbourne Mitchell and he was a charmer. However, after a good dinner, Christoph had to stop his big Mercedes on the way back to Mike's hotel so that Mike could open the door and be sick. I heard no more about Clydes!

In the salvage world no one had heard of IMS. "IM who?" people would say. They had heard of me and knew I was a professional salvor. After the arbitration, if either party did not agree with the Arbitrator's award or findings, they could appeal to the Appeal Arbitrator who was the key to the system. Mr Gerald Darling QC was the Appeal Arbitrator and had known me since I was a cadet on the "Dara". He acted for BI at the enquiry and, before becoming Appeal Arbitrator, acted for Selco on occasions. I met him at a reception during a conference on salvage and during the course of our conversation, he said, smiling, "Come a long way from being a cadet on the "Dara", *Captain* Tew. I have watched your progress with interest." Emphasis on the word 'Captain'.

I reminded Ray of this and he said, "That is all very well, he may know you but he has never heard of IMS. The important thing is to get him to recognise that IMS are professional salvors and he won't do that after only one salvage. It might take years."

We were having a leisurely dinner at Ray's hotel, discussing how best to present IMS to the salvage world, how to get us recognised as professional salvors. There was a serious monetary consideration here. Occasional or one-off salvors were not paid as much as professional salvors. The system encouraged professional salvors by paying them more, paying them in effect to have salvage tugs, equipment and personnel available at all times for salvage.

I arranged for an IMS brochure to be made with photographs and descriptions of all the tugs. We made another one of the base with all its repairs facilities and storage of salvage equipment and foam. I made a statement to Ray highlighting my involvement in salvage during the Iran-Iraq sea war and the difficulties and dangers of working in a war zone. The whole of the Gulf was now considered a war zone. The British Chamber of Commerce booklet brought out a list of all the ships hit and we had our own chart as well. I told him why I joined IMS, how I had organised the company for salvage, expanded Operations, bought the "Intergulf", hired a salvage master, placed the tugs at anchor in the gulf on salvage station.

We were professional salvors.

Ray was a top maritime lawyer, an expert in salvage law and I knew it. I was an expert in my field and he knew it. We thus had mutual respect and trust for each other and made a good team. We decided that Captain Tew, the professional salvor, would be the 'face' of IMS and I would attend all Arbitrations. There was no way we were going to be recognised as professional until we had an appeal before Gerald. Come what may, we would appeal the first award, get our evidence before him and hope he would recognise us as professional salvors and so receive enhanced awards.

The owners of the "Medusa" wanted to settle, so I agreed an acceptable figure and shortly afterwards the money marched into the IMS bank account. The eyes of Schneiders – the German accountant – opened wide when he saw the size of the settlement and he almost bowed to me. But he was the puppet of Bettermann; if Bettermann said, 'jump,' he jumped. In fact, if Bettermann had said, 'Sign this, it is your death warrant,' he would have signed. IMS were not just salvors in name, we had money as well.

"Won't help us at Arbitration to become professional if you settle," he said over the phone when I told him.

"No point antagonising a Greek owner with ships in the Gulf," I replied. "Might get another one."

But it had started and we were soon engaged in plenty of cases. Ray used every legal device to get our first arbitration heard quickly, and as soon as the award was out we appealed. We could always find some good reasons to appeal but it was important to have sound ones. The Appeal Arbitrator did not allow frivolity and he would come down like a ton of bricks if he thought we were appealing for the sake of appealing. We wanted him on our side.

In the event, the appeal arbitration went very well and he did what we had planned for. Although new salvors, we were recognised as professional, so we received an enhanced award and in the future, the Arbitrators would award us on the basis we were professional salvors. In a very short time indeed IMS had arrived on the salvage scene and was talked about in the same breath as Smits and Wjsmuller. We were no long "IM who?" but "IMS the Gulf salvors!" I was very pleased indeed and so was Ray. My grand strategy was working even better than I had hoped.

***

Mohd Saeedi was an Iranian businessman who owned a shipping agency in Tehran. I first made his acquaintance soon after the revolution when I went to Bandar Abbas on the "Salveritas" to survey a part sunken ship with a view to salvage. Mohd was in Bandar Abbas and took me round to see the various officials. The place was in a turmoil with the young revolutionary guards running around brandishing rifles. It was not a place for the faint hearted and I stood out like a sore thumb as there were no expatriates left.

The Bandar Abbas salvage did not come off but Mohd became Selco's agent in Iran. He had the most fantastic connections and always seemed to be able to obtain permission for Selco tugs to enter Iranian waters for salvage. I often spoke with him in the middle of the night. Selco kept charts of the Iranian and Iraqi 'hits' and I went to Tehran to see Mohd and negotiate with the Iranian insurance company concerning a salvage case. I was travelling light with just an overnight bag and took these two charts with me in a plastic bag. The war was raging on land and at sea. When I passed through immigration safely I thought I was home and dry. A man in plain clothes came up to me and directed me to an office. It was the revolutionary secret police whose reputation was no better than the old Shah's lot Savac. I entered clutching my plastic bag, acutely aware of the two 'hit' charts peeping over the top of my plastic bag. I broke out into a cold sweat for the first time in my life and tried to look unconcerned as I stood before my interrogator. I put the bag containing the charts between my legs. The man questioning me did not smile and had dead looking eyes. I was terrified but did my utmost not to show it, how was I to explain the charts? I was 'interrogated' for over an hour standing all the time as to why I was coming to Tehran without a visa. Obviously my answers satisfied him because he said I could go. I picked up my plastic bag with the charts sticking out, feeling as though they had a winking light on them and curbing the almost overwhelming urge to run, I walked slowly and I hoped with dignity out into the crowded, dirty, drab airport – the women veiled and dressed in black. I closed the door and started to shake with relief which, thankfully, stopped when passing through customs. Mohd was there to meet me and I told him about the encounter.

"Bad luck Tehran is dry," he laughed, "but I will buy you a good dinner." Which he did – mountains of caviar.

I felt slightly trapped; having got into Tehran, would I get out? I was completely dependent on Mohd to obtain a visa in my passport so I could leave by air. Tehran is 4,000 feet high and surrounded by mountains, snow capped until late in the year – the only colour, other than the blue sky, amongst the drab concrete buildings and brown harsh mountainsides.

We later flew down to Bushire to look at war-damaged ships, and were delayed for eight hours at the airport on our return. The Iraqis had attacked the nuclear power plant, or so we thought, but it turned out later it was probably the Israelis.

I got on well with Mohd and met him in London as well. I wanted him to be our agent for IMS but he was inclined to go with Smits, who had been after him for some time. He was owed a lot of money by Selco and had little chance of being paid. I flew to Tehran but Mohd went with Smits and so I lost my best contact in Iran.

I later flew to Tehran with Bettermann who used Salzgitter, his old company, as agents, but they did not have the entree in the salvage and tug world as Mohd, and IMS lost out as a result. However, shortly after Semco were up and running, the Iranians put out the contract for salvage in Iranian waters to tender and Semco were awarded it. IMS bid but I was a reluctant bidder once I found out the nature of the contract and I am exceedingly glad we did not get it. Semco were now inextricably linked with Iran, operating exclusively in Iranian waters, and although it excluded other salvors from entering Iranian waters, it kept them out of the rest of the Gulf. The Iranians were now attacking ships and no ship was safe anywhere in the waters of the Persian Gulf.

IMS now had a few good completed salvage operations and the money was starting to roll in. Bettermann indicated he wanted to buy more tugs and supply boats.

Gellatly Hankey, the Selco Djibouti agents, were owned by a conglomerate whose head office was in London. When I was in Djibouti salving the "Go Go Rider", the new owners were there having just removed Mr John – the old head man – and I got to know the new temporary manager, John, who was now back in London. I lunched with him quite often when I was there and he had introduced me to his boss, who was a director of Inchcape. Inchcape owned Grey Mackenzie in Bahrain and I knew they were thinking of selling their fleet. I was as keen as Bettermann to increase the size of the fleet, in fact I wanted to expand on a global basis, and I had discussed this with Bettermann in very general terms. I told him that I knew Grey Mackenzie might be for sale and he expressed great interest.

I rang London, spoke to my contact and put him in touch with Bettermann. I expected to be involved if anything became of it but Bettermann got his revenge. IMS bought the Grey Mackenzie fleet and I was totally excluded from having anything to do with it and Bettermann financed it on the back of my salvage – pledging the awards from unpaid salvage operations. Exactly what Selco had done to borrow money and contribute to the bankruptcy, for not only had the accountants borrowed against Selco's share of joint operations they had borrowed against Smits as well. I now knew there was no way I could continue working long term with the German and it was only a matter of time before I left, but not while the sea war was raging.

The war would not go on for ever and once it stopped we needed to be in place if IMS was to remain in salvage. It was fine being a Gulf salvor when there was lots of salvage, but in peace there was very little and to survive we needed to operate on a global scale. However, that dream was now shattered, and it was merely a question of biding my time.

During one of my visits to London I went to see the number three in the Mohd Al Fayed hierarchy and he listened to what I had to say about Bettermann.

"I quite agree with you but Mr Al Fayed will not hear a word against Bettermann, he is the blue-eyed boy and you are wasting your time to even try."

So that was the germ of an idea of ousting Bettermann nipped in the bud. I could have made IMS into a world class company operating on a global basis, instead it withered. Bettermann was promoted to a position in Harrods, as well as IMS and ultimately the blue-eyed boy fell from grace – but I am ahead of myself.

I continued my close relations with Smits. Soon after I arrived in Dubai Klaus Reinigert their Managing Director telephoned me and suggested a meeting, he wanted to talk about cooperation. He made regular inspection visits in the gulf and came through Dubai to meet me. The interest that Smits had in IMS was the fleet, and the interest I had in Smits was their personnel and expertise. Smits did not want to bring any more expensive Smit run tugs into the Gulf, and I needed to tap into a pool of expertise without paying for it. The obvious simple solution was to cooperate on the salvage and we came to an agreement that whichever company obtained the salvage contract they would bring in the other as co-salvor. So if IMS obtained the contract I would bring in Smits as co-salvor and vice versa. We thought it was vitally important that no one except him and I should know of any agreement. It is very difficult to keep a secret and, in the words of the American Benjamin Franklin spoken more than two hundred years ago, "Three may keep a secret, if two of them are dead."

The Arbitrators might take a dim view of it if they thought we had stitched up the Gulf and created a virtual monopoly. The counter-argument was that they might reward us for being so sensible and cooperating. However, if we asked our lawyers, or sought counsel's advice, our secret would be out, so we agreed to tell no one – and that meant no one in our own companies as well. Nothing was to be in writing and we would review the agreement at a later date. We shook hands on it and thus started a most profitable time for both our companies.

Our combined forces beat the competition in most of the

'hits' outside Iranian waters, and no one knew about our secret agreement. Louis Keyser, the Smit shore representative in Sharjah and I enjoyed a lunch once a month to review the cases we had in hand, and he must have suspected something. It became more complicated for Smits when Smit Matsas arrived on the scene, but that was not my concern.

Eventually there were so many cases that Klaus called for a meeting. I was in London and flew over to Rotterdam for the weekend on the city hopper. I was met by a car and driver and taken to Smits' headquarters by the barge harbour. It was a significant moment for me. The Dutch were the world leaders in salvage and Smits was the biggest and most successful Dutch salvor. They were the best in the world and I was entering their headquarters as a guest of the Managing Director to discuss cases where we were co-salvors, equal partners. A long, long way from chief officer of the "Salvaliant", yet only a dozen years in time, and I had only started the salvage division with IMS just over a year ago. When I left London to join Selco in Singapore, never in my wildest dreams did I imagine something like this. Just to enter the main door was to peer into salvage history – with a model of a famous Smit tug in the foyer.

Klaus had a corner office with a view over the old harbour and I spent all of Friday with him. We discussed with their in-house lawyers the cases they were dealing with, and I gave a review of the cases I was dealing with. We had agreed that if IMS had obtained the contract then I would run the case to arbitration with Elbourne Mitchel, and if Smits had obtained the contract then they would run the case with their London lawyers Holman, Fenwick & Willan. I carried a sheet with me that just contained the name of the salved ship, arbitration date, security, estimated award, tugs involved, and a one-line description of the salvage – grenade attack, fire, or whatever – and that was sufficient for me to remember all the relevant facts and be able to give an up-to-date resume. I found the legal work fascinating and had a good memory for detail and became good at assessing what a salvage was worth.

Gert Koffeman, who had been with me on the "Al Ahood"

for the cargo transfer, and was now one of Klaus's two right-hand men, ate lunch with us. Klaus was worried that, with so much money involved between the two companies, we should have the agreement in writing. It was not because he mistrusted me but if I should have an accident – say hitting a camel in the desert – then there was no proof of what we had agreed, and vice versa, say he got run over when riding his bicycle at weekends. I agreed and he produced a written agreement for me to read, which included the all-important split which was fifty fifty, irrespective of who had done what or how many tugs were involved. It was kept simple to eliminate any arguments. The only problem was that a third person knew of the agreement – the person who typed it. We agreed I would have one original and he would have another and it should remain secret. The rest of the time was spent discussing salvage, Semco, Smit Singapore office and being shown round the office. That evening at dinner we signed the agreement and I flew back the next day to London. The agreement worked smoothly until I left Dubai, when I revealed its existence to Bettermann.

Although the salvage division was more successful than I ever imagined possible, in the accounts it did not appear to be doing so well. The actual cost to IMS was me plus one other in Operations at a few hundred dollars a month, the "Intergulf" and the portable salvage equipment.

The tugs on salvage standby were charged to the marine division at a full commercial rate, so the marine division suddenly became very profitable. The net result to me was a much reduced bonus. Oh, my naivety when negotiating my contract.

The names of all the tugs and supply boats had no common denominator so, to the outside world, there was nothing to distinguish them as belonging to IMS 'that well known Gulf salvor'. We wracked our brains to come up with a solution. Selco used the Sal prefix to all the names, Smits had Smits as the prefix, what could IMS have? It was my mother who said why not use IMS and add the word Salv, so Imsalv became the prefix and we renamed all the tugs after animals consistent with their capabilities. The "Intergulf" became the "Imsalv Lion"; the other big tug became the "Imsalv Tiger"; a small but very useful boat became the "Imsalv Fox"; another one the "Imsalv Lynx" – and very successful it was too.

The final blow came when I was in England. There was an Iranian attack on the Sharjah Petroleum oil field and the storage tanker and oil production platform were set ablaze. Smits obtained the contract and IMS were the co-salvor, so Smits ran the operation.

Bettermann knew the manager and asked Klaus if he could negotiate a settlement. It was a fantastic case with very high dangers and was worth a lot of money. Just before the arbitration Bettermann finally settled but only if US$900,000 was paid back out of the settlement to Sharjah. I objected strongly because there was no need to pay them anything, we had the contract and I was certain at arbitration we would be awarded more than the settlement figure without paying anything back. All it was doing was to rob IMS of $450,000 and Smits of the same amount. For reasons I still do not know, Klaus agreed to this crazy deal. I told Bettermann I would have nothing to do with it. It later became the subject of a criminal prosecution in the Dubai Court with Bettermann in the dock.

The Iran-Iraq war stopped in July 1988 with a ceasefire and with it the salvage. Bettermann became even more difficult because he was intelligent enough to see that when the cases were through arbitration, the salvage income would stop and IMS would suddenly become not so profitable, if not unprofitable, and no provision had been made for the future. My grand vision was out of the window because I could no longer work with the German and the sooner I left the better, but first I wanted my money.

I stayed on for another nine months, attending arbitrations in London. I once flew to Tokyo and negotiated a fantastic settlement with the Japanese on one of the last ships hit in the Gulf. I prepared myself properly and had a case full of documents which I used to answer the questions put by the committee of six confronting me. I was very pleased with myself and so were Smits.

It was with great relief after my last day with IMS I flew to Mauritius in the Indian Ocean for a holiday, sailing hobby catamarans in the lagoon near the hotel by day and gambling in the casino at night. I flew home via Nairobi, where I went on safari with my mother who arrived from England.

UK ALDERNEY RIO DUBAI

I was back in England for the summer, a 'free' man with enough money to do nothing for a while, although there was cloud faintly on the horizon. It was 1989 and the first very faint rumblings of trouble at Lloyds was being heard – asbestos and pollution. However, I received a cheque for the 1986 account and bought a shop with two flats above it in Alderney, the northernmost Channel Island. I spent some time looking for a suitable boat. I chartered a Freedom 21, test sailing her for ten days in the West Country. I found she was a young man's boat and I was no longer young, but coming up to middle-age! I finally settled on a Freedom 30, "Freedom Freyja" (Freyja is the Swedish Goddess of love) and sailed off single handed to Brittany for the remaining summer. I spent two and a half months on my own and wrote up the Log for the RCC Journal, which was published. I kept the boat at the Beaucette marina in Guernsey over the winter.

Peter Bruce rang me up one day in October from Australia and suggested I might like Rio de Janeiro for a change of scene. I agreed and flew out with US$40,000 in cash secreted around my body, which I picked up at Heathrow Airport from Thomas Cook. I was supposed to get a tanker ready for sailing to India for scrap. It was with much relief that I put the money in the safe of the Meridien Copacabana, where I lived for three months. I am ashamed to say I was not very successful, having spent too much time in the night clubs. I flew home after Peter turned up to relieve me.

I spent an unsatisfactory few months doing nothing when Mohd Saeedi rang up and asked me to go back to Dubai and work for him. I saw him in London with his right-hand man Christian Bang, and flew to Dubai. Saddam Hussein invaded Kuwait shortly afterwards. I was in Singapore at the time looking at the tug Mohd had purchased. I flew back to Dubai in an almost empty plane to find Dubai with a much reduced expatriate community. I spent six unsatisfactory months in Dubai and went to Sri Lanka for Christmas 1990. I was not very well and flew back to England on New Year's Eve.

The Gulf War was fought and won but I did not return to work in Dubai. The rumblings at Lloyds became fact and I faced huge losses, which I did not think I was in a position to pay, despite my Godmother dying and leaving me some money. I sailed "Freedom Freyja" back to England and a mooring on the Beaulieu River down by the Beaulieu River Sailing Club, of which I was a member.

The disaster at Lloyds seemed to be getting worse so I started a shop on the Quay at Lymington in November 1991 selling nautical clocks, barometers and books – not that I expected to make a fortune but it gave me a cash flow and time to think what to do about Lloyds.

It was quite like old times when the limo pulled up at 04:00 in the morning to take me to Gatwick for the Emirates flight to Dubai. The club class flight was as good as ever with excellent food, and it was a clear day so I was able to look at the view from my window seat. It was the first flight I had made for 18 months and I was quite excited – and this from someone who had flown over a million miles in ten years!

I was met at the airport by one of the IMS drivers, who brought me up to date with the news. Bettermann, of course, had gone; as had his secretary, Judith; Omar was still there, what a survivor he was; Adnam was vice-president; and an Arab banker was president. The office and base had been moved to Jabal Ali, the huge port half an hour's drive from the creek.

"No excitement now, sir, no salvage," the driver said with a grin, turning to look at me sitting in the back.

My old secretary, Dominic, was still there but worked in the passport section; Gordon still repaired the boats and worked from an office at Al Jadaf, the repair yard above the road bridge over the creek.

The driver dropped me off at the Sheraton Hotel. The balcony from my room overlooked the creek, and just downstream on the opposite side was a bare piece of land. It had been the IMS base and nothing was left. The place – with all its heartache, all its triumph – was just a memory.

A driver and car was assigned to me each day so I could go anywhere, which was very pleasant. Dubai was all hustle and bustle, the roads were choked with traffic, new buildings were going up, the place was busy. The climate was hot but not unbearably so and after November in England was bliss.

Omar took me to see the IMS Dubai lawyers where I made a statement concerning my role in IMS and the events surrounding the payback of US$900,000. On another day he took me to see the Dubai prosecutor who was prosecuting Bettermann. I would be appearing in court one day next week, meanwhile enjoy Dubai. I did!

I was in Dubai for over a month so made good use of the car and driver. I was driven across the desert to a small hotel in the foothills of the mountains for a swim and lunch. We went to Al Ain, the university town of the Emirates, which is in foothills of the mountains near the border with Abu Dhabi. It takes two and a half hours of desert driving to reach Abu Dhabi but I was not doing the driving so it was fun.

I met up with Barry Howard, the actor, who lived in Bournemouth and drove him to Fujairah to swim in the blue Arabian Sea and have lunch. The entry to the town is spectacular, the road having been cut through the barren mountains.

The Dubai Courthouse is an imposing building. It was beginning to get hot when we arrived at the large car park. Omar and I met up with the IMS lawyers and we went into the courtroom at the appointed time. I entered with considerable trepidation; an Arab country, strange law, and I was an alien.

Ahead of me was a raised dias. In the belly of the court were benches which were already filled with people. To the right of the dias was a cage with bars, just like the cage for a wild animal in a zoo. It was filled with people standing, and in the front was Bettermann. It was a real shock, a culture shock, to see anyone in a cage let alone the proud German I had worked for. He looked pale and thinner than when I last saw him.

The Dubai prosecutor came in dressed in a red cape,

obviously designed to intimidate, and stood at a small desk on the left-hand side of the dias. Three judges came in and the court stood while they took their seats on the raised dias, looking down on all in the court. In the middle of the court, at the front under the very noses of the judges, was the witness box.

I took a deep breath as I was led to the box and the door closed behind me – all eyes in the court, including the judges', on me. There then ensued a legal argument in Arabic about the interpreter, which gave me a chance to settle down and get my heart beat down. Once the argument was over the Dubai prosecutor asked me questions in Arabic, which were then translated into English, along the lines of the statement I had made. I answered in English in what I hoped was a clear steady voice.

Bettermann's lawyer objected every now and then, mainly over the translation. The translation gave me lots of time to think and remember what I said in my statement. I gave my evidence truthfully and honestly. Bettermann was yesterday's story as far as I was concerned and much as I might have disliked him at the time I was working for IMS, he was history so I did not try and slant my evidence against him. Suddenly it was over, next case. I had to return the next week and answer more questions.

It was very hot back out in the car park and I looked forward to a swim at the Sheraton to unwind.

I appeared four times in the court and spent nine hours in the witness box, and then flew home for the rest of the UK winter. Almost a year later I found out that the three judges were changed and Bettermann was acquitted.

UK SHOP

I went to London a lot and took part in meetings of Lloyds Names and joined three action groups. These were dark days indeed; I faced bankruptcy or, later, going to see Mary Archer on the hardship committee.

In 1993 I pledged everything I owned to Lloyds and increased my underwriting. If I was going to go bust I was going to go bust with a bang. My brother James was employed in London with a company engaged in esoteric work to do with investment. I was advised on a good investment by a Mr Evans of Grimston Scott, and James came with me to interview the fund manager. He pronounced the investment as sound and it did very well indeed, so well in fact that I sold out and had money in the bank!

The shop was quite successful as a one-man project, but a tremendous bind. I could not sell anything if the shop was shut. It was fascinating to be behind a shop counter and observe human behaviour. To some I was just a shop worker of no significance thus treated as such with anonymity, or in some cases with superciliousness, others engaged me in conversation and turned out to be interesting people; and others were browsers who had no intention of buying anything. These I found the most difficult because it was *my* goods they were playing with which, of course, is the wrong attitude to have as a shopkeeper.

One 'browser' managed to annoy me enough so I asked him if he was going to buy anything or not and he replied, "No, I cannot afford to and it is all very well for you living in a nice place surrounded by fascinating things. I live in Birmingham and I work in a factory and it is a treat for me to be here." I tried to be more tolerant in the future.

Soon after starting the shop Wendy turned up asking for a job and she became very helpful doing odd hours for me and days when I went to London. Wendy was a well-known

Lymington character, full of fun and non-stop chatter, with an unmistakable hairstyle. Much more importantly she was good in a boat. When I found help for the shop, she came day sailing with me.

We crossed the Channel to Cherbourg and had the best sail back I ever enjoyed in "Frejya", averaging just over six knots on a broad reach with bright sunshine. Our record for non-stop chatter was nine hours!

In the winter of 1994 I flew to Hong Kong with a Chinese friend and did a three week tour in China, which was fascinating. I flew on to Sydney and stayed with Peter Bruce and his wife, being confined to the house for four days during the bush fires. Los Angeles fell down in the earthquake on the day I rang to confirm my booking to San Francisco. The insurance losses turned out larger than expected and impacted on a few of my syndicates.

During the dead months of 1996 January and February, I flew to Singapore and was taken by a friend to see the old Selco base. It was very eerie and poignant. The 'new' office block was empty and deserted. Mr Kahlenberg's office in the old one-storey building was now part of a warehouse. The shipyard had gone downhill and in my head I could hear the voices of Selco personnel. All the sweat and toil, the successes and failure, all gone into the ether – all but a memory.

Kahlenberg had died and few attended his funeral; Patani, my old bosun, drowned; Diotay, my old Salvaliant cook, dead from cirrhosis of the liver; Barros, my "Salvanguard" bosun, killed in the Gulf War; as was my Chinese cadet; and my "Salvanguard" messman killed when an Exocet hit the engine room of a ship they were salving. The only sign that Selco ever existed was on the electricity shed, which had a Selco shipyard sign on it. It was history; the past, it was gone – look to the future.

I found someone to look after the shop and spent a good deal of the summer of 1996 sailing. Edward and I sailed "Freyja" to Ireland and back in 12 days, and were awarded the RCC Royal Cork vase and the account was published in the Journal. I later sailed down to the Morbihan in the Bay of Biscay and back with Michael, an Irishman I met who took to the sea like a duck to the water.

In November I moved the shop to larger premises with Paul who now joined me on a permanent basis. Paul was cheerful and really good at displays, especially the window. I thought I could make a display but by altering just a few angles, good became brilliant. I now worked with a fully fledged deal with Nauticalia and the shop became a sort of franchise, although still mine. We were still on the Quay but now in the most prominent position, and once Chris Murdoch from Nauticalia refitted the premises they stood out and attracted the eye.

The coastal erosion at Thorns Beach where my mother still lived became so bad that remedial work had to be carried out or the sea would break through. Beaulieu Estate, who owned the beach, would not admit any liability, although Lord Montagu admitted a moral duty. In the end I worked out a deal with them whereby Beaulieu supplied the timber and I supplied the labour. The work was much delayed in starting but luckily the winter produced mostly easterly gales so little more was lost. However, just supplying the labour was expensive and I borrowed money from Midlands and credit cards to pay.

Ralph Montagu wanted to buy the Windmill but would not offer enough money. Then he was offered a lease but eventually it was put on the market and sold very well. All debts were paid off and my mother owned a bit more capital.

On Christmas Eve 1996 I received the first of my Lloyds profits and what a relief it was. My assets were now mine and I had profits to boot, having paid all my losses. The future looked rosy again and I allowed a seed to germinate. I bought yachting magazines and started to look at boats.

Finally M, whom I met in London, turned up out of the blue and I asked him, "Do you want to sail round the world with me?"

The almost immediate reply was "Yes."

M was the catalyst. We looked at and almost bought a Freedom 35 but after the survey turned her down.

Peter Bruce rang up out of the blue and I drove down to

Plymouth. He was getting an RFA tanker ready to sail to India for scrap and wanted me to take her as master. I thought about it but I owned the shop and my sailing. It was putting the clock back not forwards so I declined.

CIRCUMNAVIGATION

On 12 October 1997 M and I took over "Independent Freedom" at the municipal marina near Sandy Hook and sailed to New York. I sorted out a problem with the customs at their headquarters at Newark and we sailed south.

I wrote up our shake down cruise to Cambridge Chesapeake Bay, which was published in the RCC Journal.

The Intercoastal Waterway was hard motoring and hard work but it got us down the 1,100 statute miles to Fort Lauderdale in sheltered waters for I did not fancy the winter North Atlantic in a small boat. Both my elder brother Donald and my grandfather were caught out in Atlantic winter storms, and I had no desire to be the third in my family.

M and I initiated many repairs and improvements including importing a self steering gear from Canada. An SBS radio and transmitter was fitted as well and the flexy aerial fitted right aft. The marina was so huge we hired a car so we could reach the loo without a long walk especially if it was raining.

M had a court date in Ireland and flew home, while I flew to England for a couple of weeks and saw my aunt who sailed with her father across the Pacific just before the War. It was the beginning of my proposed book.

Edward and Philippa and my Goddaughter, Camilla, and her sister, Olivia, came out to Nassau, Bahamas for Christmas, leaving in Georgetown on New Years's Eve.

M and I continued on to Cuba, Cayman Islands, and through the Panama Canal into the Pacific, where we followed in the wake of my grandfather almost fifty-nine years after him.

Tahiti, August 1998

AFTERWORD

This memoir was written entirely from memory while stranded in Tahiti, engineless, waiting for a new one to be flown up from Auckland. Any inaccuracies are completely due to my memory. It was an interesting and stimulating project necessary to keep me reasonably on the straight and narrow from the temptations of this exotic and erotic island. My crew enjoyed Tahiti one way or another and made friends with an American yacht in the marina. I am astonished at the amount remembered for now I require a prompt. There was a time limit, the hurricane season was approaching and as soon as the engine arrived and was fitted we would sail. The two months spent writing more than one thousand words a day was very intense as I rushed through what turned out to be a varied and interesting life although there is often a lack of detail. It is more a cameo than an in depth biography.

Tiggs, Nick's Boston terrier, is snoring as I write this afterword some twenty years later in my office looking out over a field towards the Isle of Wight, the glint of the Solent just visible at high water.

The twenty years, apart from the first two, have not been so eventful although nothing could match the salvage years but the years have been very different. Running the shop was mundane although Lloyds was high risk and for the second time in my life I faced bankruptcy but pulled through and now I am out. I have been around the world again but that was as a fee paying passenger amongst many on a ship so does not really count. I have been to Antarctica and that was really interesting there being only a hundred or so fellow travellers and we landed in rubber boats.

"Sailing in Grandfather's Wake" my account of the circumnavigation of the world with "Independent Freedom" was published by Reeds in 2001 the year we returned to the UK. "Salvage A Personal Odyssey" my account of my salvage years was published in 2007 by Seafarers. I have just published a novel about about salvage "The Dare" and two books of short stories "Reflections on The Sea," so I have not been entirely idle. The shop is long gone and is now a cafe although still called "The Boathouse."

I shared for a few years a beautiful Nicholson forty ketch, "Coral of Aqaba," with my brothers after being forced to sell "Independent Freedom." We made some good cruises including Scotland. Disease has forced me to abandon the sea but I have enjoyed six years cruising the English inland waterways with Nick and our sixty foot narrow boat, "Merlot", but now we have been forced to sell her because I can no longer get onboard.

The sea, the sea, oh the sea, her call has left me. I never thought in my wildest dreams she would go and she has and taken part of my soul with her. My earliest memories are of the sea, the harbour waters of Poole lapping on the shore in front of our house Waterfront. The sound of the wind at sea from those earliest times to the almost insensate howl of a typhoon, the sea hissing, to the gentle hum of a breeze in the rigging running before the trade winds. Never will I forget the sensation of speed as Edward and I as teenagers overtook the Yarmouth Lymington ferry in my firefly testing the new self bailers, invincible, immortal youth, at one with the boat and the sea, we felt as though we were flying jumping from wave to wave. The sensation, so different in "Independent Freedom" flying up the Red Sea with stark barren Abu Ail behind us, the wind a steady fifty knots as we surged and surfed northwards. And so many others to be remembered. The sea in all her states from ice like calm, silver in the moonlight, to the white topped breaking waves seemingly hurling themselves at yacht or ship, to the glint of the dancing sea in bright sunshine or the grey northern seas dull under grey low cloud where the sun seems lost, to the bright tropical seas so clear you can see into the depths, even her very soul, never forgetting the sea is a demanding mistress at all times requiring respect or she will kill you. My living was made on the sea, my greatest pleasures have been sailing on the sea, my inspiration has come from the sea, the very reason to live has been the sea, and now it seems she has deserted me and left me bereft.

THE END

Printed in Great Britain
by Amazon